CAMPAIGN 423

HANSANDO AND BUSAN 1592

Admiral Yi Sun-sin's First Victories against Japan

YUHAN KIM　　　　ILLUSTRATED BY DARREN TAN

OSPREY PUBLISHING
Bloomsbury Publishing Plc
Kemp House, Chawley Park, Cumnor Hill, Oxford OX2 9PH, UK
Bloomsbury Publishing Ireland Limited,
29 Earlsfort Terrace, Dublin 2, D02 AY28, Ireland
1385 Broadway, 5th Floor, New York, NY 10018, USA
E-mail: info@ospreypublishing.com
www.ospreypublishing.com

OSPREY is a trademark of Osprey Publishing Ltd

First published in Great Britain in 2025

© Osprey Publishing Ltd, 2025

All rights reserved. No part of this publication may be: i) reproduced or transmitted in any form, electronic or mechanical, including photocopying, recording or by means of any information storage or retrieval system without prior permission in writing from the publishers; or ii) used or reproduced in any way for the training, development or operation of artificial intelligence (AI) technologies, including generative AI technologies. The rights holders expressly reserve this publication from the text and data mining exception as per Article 4(3) of the Digital Single Market Directive (EU) 2019/790

A catalogue record for this book is available from the British Library.

ISBN: PB 9781472868862; eBook 9781472868879; ePDF 9781472868848; XML 9781472868855

25 26 27 28 29   10 9 8 7 6 5 4 3 2 1

Maps by Bounford.com
3D BEVs by Paul Kime
Index by Mark Swift
Typeset by Lumina Datamatics Ltd
Printed by Repro India Ltd

Osprey Publishing supports the Woodland Trust, the UK's leading woodland conservation charity.

To find out more about our authors and books visit www.ospreypublishing.com. Here you will find extracts, author interviews, details of forthcoming events and the option to sign up for our newsletter.

For product safety related questions contact productsafety@bloomsbury.com

Acknowledgements

Many people contributed to the writing of this book to whom I owe thanks, including Professor Nam-lin Hur, who kindly lent me his wisdom and knowledge on the Imjin War and the staff of the various museums across Japan and South Korea who provided me with the materials that went into this book, in particular Director Kim Min-su of the Okpo Battle Memorial Park. Thank you to Osprey editors Brianne Bellio and Alexandra Boulton for their guidance and support for this book. I am grateful to my friends Cole Snedeker and Julian Daniel who took the time to look over my manuscript, to Anna Zhao for assisting with translation, to Yeji Kim, Hyun-sung Kim, Major Seung-jin hong, Jack He and Satoshi Yanaizu for connecting me to museums in Japan and South Korea, and to all those who provided me with encouragement. Finally, I am grateful to my family for assisting me with research and supporting me in my endeavours.

Notes

This book uses the Korean lunar calendar for dates (X day X month; Xd Xm), as was used at the time of the Imjin War and is done in many secondary works. The Korean lunar calendar operates similarly to the Gregorian calendar; the only major differences are that it runs about a month behind, there are 29–30 days in each month and there is an extra month every three years. Korean names and locations are spelled based on the Revised Romanization System, unless they are more commonly known by the McCune–Reischauer Romanization.

There were two men by the name of Yi Sun-sin serving as ranking officers in the Jeolla Left Navy. The *Cheomsa* (deputy commander) Yi Sun-sin is distinguished from the Admiral Yi Sun-sin by reference to the former's posthumous title (Muui-gong; denoted as M). In the Korean language, the suffix '-san' refers to a mountain and '-do' refers to an island.

Quotations are primarily drawn from Yi's diary (the *Nanjung Ilgi*), the *Imjin Changjo* or the Joseon *Sillok* (royal records).

Front cover main illustration: The battle of Dangpo, 2d 6m 1592. (Darren Tan)
Title page photograph: The battle of Hansando, 8d 7m 1592. (From the War Memorial of Korea)

CONTENTS

ORIGINS OF THE CAMPAIGN 4

CHRONOLOGY 8

OPPOSING COMMANDERS 10
Joseon ▪ Japanese

OPPOSING FORCES 24
Joseon ▪ Japanese

THE CAMPAIGNS 37
The first campaign: Okpo ▪ The second campaign: Sacheon, Dangpo and Danghangpo ▪ The third campaign: Hansando and Angolpo ▪ The fourth campaign: Busan ▪ The fifth campaign: Ungpo

AFTERMATH 83
Analysis and impact

THE BATTLEFIELDS TODAY 89

BIBLIOGRAPHY 93

INDEX 95

ORIGINS OF THE CAMPAIGN

Print of Konishi Yukinaga by Ochiai Yoshiiku. Konishi Yukinaga led the vanguard of the invasion force (1st Division) and became the premier Japanese commander in the Imjin War. He developed an intense rivalry with 2nd Division commander Kato Kiyomasa, but was unmatched as the most capable Japanese field commander in the war. He oversaw Japan's negotiations with Ming China during the 1594–96 stalemate. At the renewal of hostilities, Konishi commanded the Japanese fortress at Suncheon, whose relief became the focal point of the final climactic naval battle at Noryang. Fighting for the losing side at Sekigahara, he refused to commit *seppuku* due to his Catholic faith and was executed instead. (From the Tokyo Metropolitan Library)

On the evening of 13d 4m (23 May) 1592,[1] hundreds of sails appeared on the horizon before the city of Busan in Gyeongsang Province, on the south-east tip of the Korean Peninsula. The city garrison and civilians who crowded the harbour and walls watched with trepidation, uncertain if this fleet was a large party of merchants, a bold pirate raid or the long-rumoured Japanese invasion. It must have been a long night for those in Busan, and a sleepless one with a foreign armada hovering just outside. At dawn the next morning, thousands of samurai and ashigaru from Konishi Yukinaga's 1st Division leapt from the boats and waded ashore. The garrison commander of Busan, Jeong Bal, clad in black armour, ordered his musicians to play to calm the civilians as he finalized the defences. Numbering 158,800 men in all, the host before Busan was the largest amphibious invasion force the early modern world had seen.

Jeong Bal and his 800 men, aided by civilian militia, put up a magnificent defence, braving the suppressive fire of Japanese arquebusiers to knock down ladders and fire their own arrows in return. They held out for hours, but the Japanese broke through the weaker northern side of the castle. By 1400hrs, the castle had fallen and the entire garrison lay dead. The Japanese troops then went on a rampage inside Busan, sacking the city and killing nearly every living thing they found – not even dogs were spared, according to Korean accounts. For the Joseon kingdom (Korean ruling dynasty of 1392–1897), the slaughter at Busan was but a taste of the seven-year conflict known as the

Imjin War, which would ravage the Korean Peninsula and leave over a million dead. It would weaken two dynasties and bring them closer to their downfall, while leaving a third war-torn and impoverished for decades. For the Japanese, the desperate and fanatical resistance of Jeong Bal and his entourage at Busan was a foreshadowing of things to come – Jeong Bal and his men died making a final stand, his concubine Ae-hyang committed suicide over his body and her servant Yong-wol also died charging the Japanese in the streets. It was clear from the start that the long war in Korea would bleed the Japanese divisions dry.

The architect of the invasion was Toyotomi Hideyoshi, the Taiko (regent) of Japan. A young Hideyoshi, who had been a nameless *ashigaru* (Japanese feudal infantry) grunt just 34 years previously, could hardly have imagined his position as ruler of Japan in 1592. Through incredible ambition and ability, he had clawed his way

---

1   See page 2 for information on the Korean lunar calendar.

up the ladder of Japanese society, rising beyond his means to become a powerful *daimyo* (feudal lord), and eventually unifying the warring clans of Japan under his rule. Hideyoshi's exact reasons for invading Korea are still debated to this day. Some historians believe that the ambitious Hideyoshi sought to conquer Ming China, and the Korean Peninsula was just a highway to his grand plan. Others, such as historian Nam-lin Hur, suggest that Hideyoshi's objectives were limited to a campaign in Korea, with his true goal being to instigate an external conflict to consolidate his tenuous hold over Japan's clans.

Studying the course of the war leaves the impression that Hideyoshi's invasion was one that teetered on the brink of failure in its initial stages. The Korean navy was far superior in terms of weaponry and tactics over anything the Japanese could field. At any point in the crucial hours between the Japanese armada's departure from Tsushima to its arrival in Busan, the tide of history could have been turned by a sortie of the Joseon navy. But no such event occurred, and the Japanese expeditionary force carried on northwards, making a blitz for the Joseon capital of Hanyang (modern-day Seoul). They shattered every army they encountered, and history played its course. Admiral Yi Sun-sin, too, asks this question throughout his reports and in his diaries, lamenting the possibility that the invasion could have been stopped at sea considering the weakness of the Japanese navy. This begs the question, where was the Joseon fleet when the Japanese landed at Busan?

The Japanese landed in the zone of operation of the Gyeongsang Left Navy, commanded by Park Hong. Park has been scapegoated as the man who failed to stop the invasion, even more so because he ultimately ordered the Gyeongsang Left Navy to be scuttled. Gyeongsang *Choyusa* (military commissioner tasked with organizing guerrillas) Kim Song-il complained:

> Left Naval Commander Park Hong abandoned the castle first without firing a single arrow, the Left Military Commander Lee Gak fled to Dongnae Castle afterwards, the Right Military Commander Jo Daegon was old and fearful and always retreated and cowered, and the Right Naval Commander Won Gyun burned the camp and went out to sea, preserving only one ship. When soldiers and naval commanders are the leaders of a province and act like this, how could the officers and men under their command not flee or scatter?

The truth was that the troops in Busan and the surrounding castles put up a fierce resistance that delayed the Japanese advance. To explain the scuttling of the Gyeongsang Left Navy as an act of cowardice or insanity would be a betrayal of Park's stellar record in the Joseon military thus far. When the shooting started, Park assembled what naval troops he had on hand and attempted to break through to Dongnae Castle. Failing to do so, he retreated, and scuttled the ships under his command. There are several reasons why Park may have done this.

The *Memorial to the Busanjin Martyrs* was first painted in 1709, but it had become so faded over time that it was repainted in 1760 by Byeon Bak, a *Jaeji Hwawon* (local government painter) in Dongraebu (Dongnae). Under the central gate pavilion is Jeong Bal in his black armor, and further behind him is the governor's residence, where Ae-hyang and her retainers wait armed. The Japanese troops are depicted in simple garbs in contrast to the detailed uniforms of the Busan garrison, suggesting the sheer numbers of troops and ships as the defenders of Busan would have seen. The painting also shows the Japanese landing off barges with front ramps. There is no record of the Japanese designing special landing craft for direct amphibious assault. Rather, they probably rowed troops onto the beach in small boats. (Courtesy of Kang Han-eul, Korea Army Museum)

In 1783, Byeon Bak painted the *Memorial to the Dongnae Castle Martyrs*. Byeong's painting is nearly identical to a 1658 painting by Min Jeong-jung, who based his painting on the testimony of a survivor from the battle. Dongnae Castle was a mountain castle 10km north of Busan, defending the road to Hanyang. Konishi Yukinaga's division attacked it on 15d 4m at 0800hrs. After many hours of desperate fighting, the Japanese managed to scale the castle walls. Knowing their fate, many civilians fought the Japanese in the streets, throwing roof tiles and meeting *katanas* with farm implements. Thousands were massacred as the castle fell. Forensic research of a mass grave in the old castle moat discovered in 2005 revealed horrific blunt force trauma injuries on the remains of toddlers and women. The mounted figure in the upper left corner is the commander of the Gyeongsang Left Army, Lee Gak, who fled despite being the senior Joseon commander on the scene. He was later executed for desertion. (Courtesy of Kang Han-eul, Korea Army Museum)

First, the Joseon fleets were not kept in a state of war-readiness at all times. Only a fraction of the sailors were on base, as they were conscripted farmers. The squadrons that made up a provincial fleet were not kept in one large harbour, but scattered across many miles at different civilian and military ports. Seeing the length of time it took for the Jeolla Province navies to assemble, it is clear that the Joseon navy was not a rapid-response force, at either an organizational or command level, nor does it seem to be one that rewarded initiative – even Yi Sun-sin, an opportunistic and aggressive officer in his youth, delayed sailing out until he had received official orders to do so.

Second, Joseon preparations for a war against Japan were also founded on a gross overestimation of Japanese naval capabilities. Jeong Bal, upon seeing the Japanese fleet, scuttled the three ships under his command and ordered his men into the castle, instead of trying to fight a naval battle. Park was likely caught in a dilemma – to charge the hundreds of Japanese ships with the few dozen he had would be a glorious suicide, while to pull them back would be seen as an act of cowardice. Yi argued that Park should have at least done something with his ships, such as inflicting as much damage as he could. But Park was no Yi, who had the nerves and death-defying courage to fight against insurmountable odds.

Third, the Joseon military had few career navy men – its officers frequently rotated between the two branches, so it makes sense from a perspective of personal experience that Park tried to move his troops to fight in a fortified position at Dongnae Castle. Lee Eon-ham, the magistrate of the naval county of Ulsan, also retreated to a castle instead of trying to assemble his ships.

It is unlikely that the Joseon navy could ever have defeated Hideyoshi's invasion at Busan barring a massive intelligence leak days in advance. But we only have to look to the German perspective on Operation *Overlord* to see the immense difficulty of anticipating the date and location of a mass amphibious assault. A preemptive strike against Tsushima would have required royal permission, a process that would have taken more precious days. However, Park had a full night between the arrival of the Japanese navy and the outbreak of violence. Even if this was not long enough to assemble the full fleet, a man with greater foresight and naval sense would have relayed orders for the port captains to fall back to a rally point in another province to fight another day.

The Japanese invasion, 13d 4m–14d 6m

1. After taking Busan and the surrounding castles, the Japanese army marches north, spearheaded by the divisions of Konishi Yukinaga and Kato Kiyomasa.
2. At the battle of Chungju (28d 4m), a Joseon army of mostly cavalry under Sin Rip is defeated by Konishi Yukinaga.
3. The Japanese advance and capture Hanyang on 2d 5m, while King Seonjo and his court flee north.
4. The Joseon army attempts to retake Hanyang, but is defeated at the battle of the Imjin River (18d 5m).
5. With nothing standing in their way, the Japanese advance to Pyongyang, while King Seonjo flees even further north. Pyongyang falls on 14d 6m.

CHRONOLOGY

1592

13d 4m, lunar calendar (23 May, Gregorian calendar)	Konishi Yukinaga's 1st Division departs from Tsushima
13d 4m (23 May)	The Japanese fleet arrives at Busan
13–14d 4m (23–24 May)	The battle of Busan – Konishi's troops storm and sack the city
15d 4m (25 May)	The battle of Dongnae – Dongnae Castle falls to the Japanese
28d 4m (7 June)	The battle of Chungju – a Joseon army under Sin Rip is defeated by Konishi
2d 5m (11 June)	Hanyang falls to the Japanese
7d 5m (16 June)	The battles of Okpo and Happo (Yi's first campaign)
8d 5m (17 June)	The battle of Jeokjinpo (Yi's first campaign)
18d 5m (27 June)	The battle of the Imjin River – the Joseon army launches a failed counterattack across the Imjin River against Kato Kiyomasa
29d 5m (8 July)	The battle of Sacheon (Yi's second campaign)
2d 6m (10 July)	The battle of Dangpo (Yi's second campaign)
5d 6m (13 July)	The battle of Danghangpo (Yi's second campaign)
5–6d 6m (13–14 July)	The battle of Yongin – Wakizaka Yasuharu defeats an army from Jeolla Province that was attempting to retake Hanyang
7d 6m (15 July)	The battle of Yulpo (Yi's second campaign)
14d 6m (22 July)	Pyongyang falls
7d 7m (13 August)	The battle of Ungchi (Jeolla campaign)
8d 7m (14 August)	The battle of Ichi (Jeolla campaign)
9–10d 7m (15–16 August)	The first battle of Geumsan Mountain (Jeolla campaign)
18d 8m (23 September)	The second battle of Geumsan Mountain (Jeolla campaign)
8d 7m (14 August)	The battle of Hansando (Yi's third campaign)
10d 7m (16 August)	The battle of Angolpo (Yi's third campaign)

29d 8m (4 October)	The battle of Janglimpo (Yi's fourth campaign)
1d 9m (5 October)	The battles of Hwajun-Gumi, Dadepo, Seopyeongpo, Jeolyeongdo, Choryangmok and Busan (Yi's fourth campaign)
4–10d 10m (7–13 November)	The first siege of Jinju – the Jinju garrison under Kim Si-min successfully repels waves of relentless Japanese assaults

1593

6–9d 1m (6–9 February)	The fourth battle of Pyongyang – Ming and Joseon troops force Konishi Yukinaga from Pyongyang
27d 1m (27 February)	The battle of Byeokjegwan – Ming force moving on Hanyang is defeated
10d 2m–3d 4m (12 March–3 May)	The Ungpo campaign (Yi's fifth campaign)
12d 2m (14 March)	The battle of Haengju – Kwon Yul defeats Ukita Hideie in a defensive battle
21–29d 6m (19–27 July)	The second siege of Jinju – a Japanese army of 90,000 men besieges and destroys Jinju fortress

The iron kettle helmet was popular among Joseon troops, as it was cheaper than the *dujeonggap* helmet. This particular example was found at the aforementioned mass grave at Dongnae Castle. Three hanja (Chinese characters for written Korean) characters are punched into the rim, which has rusted over time, but enough is left to discern that it spelled '東萊鎮上', meaning 'Dongnae Garrison Front/First'. '上' was possibly used to indicate a subunit of the garrison. (From the collection of the Busan Metropolitan Museum, accessible at https://www.emuseum.go.kr/)

OPPOSING COMMANDERS

JOSEON

Military structure

The Joseon military was a complex bureaucratic organization that merits understanding before any explanation of its personnel or the conflicts it fought. Joseon society was organized on a caste-like system with the *yangban* Confucian scholar aristocracy at the top. The primary role of the yangban class was to produce the personnel that ran the Joseon state apparatus. Yangban men, under great social pressure to do so, entered state service by taking either the civil exam to become bureaucrats (*munban*) or the military exam to become officers (*muban*). There were few career alternatives for yangban men who failed to become civil servants – the great guerrilla leader Kwak Jae-u had been languishing at home in early retirement since 1585 after passing the exam but being blacklisted because he criticized government policies.

While commoners were in theory allowed to take the exam, nearly all those who passed were yangban, as only they had the financial security to commit to the years and years of preparation needed. The military exam, the Siknyeonsi, was held every three years, with only the top 28 scorers passing. It was a truly difficult exam. There were local qualifier exams held in each province, then an intermediary at the capital of Hanyang and, finally, a palace examination, held before the king himself. Candidates were tested on equestrian skills, spear combat and archery. Particular emphasis was placed on the latter, which took up as much as half of the 90-minute physical exam. In the final stage of the exam, candidates were tested on their knowledge of military classics and strategy. The passing class of 28 was classified into A (top three scorers), B (next five) and C (remaining 20) officers. Nonetheless, the civil exam was regarded as more prestigious, so the Joseon military often made do with yangban who were only there because they had failed to pass the civil exam.

Joseon military command was structured such that provincial military commands followed orders from a central command that answered to the king. Each province was divided into two military administrations, Left (eastern) and Right (western), each having their own army and navy commanders (the left and right was denominated from the perspective of the king when he looked south from Hanyang). The governor of a province sometimes doubled for one of the military roles. Joseon officers and officials were divided into 18 ranks, from 1A to 9B.

Naval ranks and commands in Jeolla and Gyeongsang provinces at the time of the Imjin War

Joseon naval officer rank	Jeolla Province positions		Gyeongsang Province positions	
Jeoldosa (fleet commander/admiral): 3A officer in charge of fleet management and command of all the port garrisons. One Jeoldosa concurrently held the position of Governor	Governor Jeolla Left Navy Jeoldosa (main base at Naeryepo, better known as Yeosu) Jeolla Right Navy Jeoldosa (main base at Juryang) Jeju Island Army – Navy Liaison Commander		Governor Gyeongsang Left Navy Jeoldosa (main base at Haeeunpo) Gyeongsang Right Navy Jeoldosa (main base at Oipo)	
Cheomsa (deputy commander): 3B rank officer in command of a naval base	Sadojin Cheomsa (Left) Imchidojin Cheomsa (Right)		Busanjin Cheomsa (Left) Jepojin Cheomsa (Right)	
Uhu (staff adjutant captain): 4A officer that acted as an assistant to the Jeoldosa	One		Two each for Left and Right navies	
Manho (port captain): commander of ships at a port station, equivalent to a flotilla or squadron commander	Left Navy Sado Bangdap Yeodo Nokdo Balpo	Right Navy Imchi Gyeommopo Dakyungpo Geunsanpo Mokpo Beopseongpo Namdopo Garipo Uhrinpo Hwaryangpo Geumgapdo Ijin Mado	Left Navy Busanpo Dadepo Seosaengpo Gampo Dumopo Chilpo Chuksanpo Poipo Seopyeongpo Gaeeunpo	Right Navy Gabaeryang Jepo Yeongdeungpo Jeokryang Okpo Pyeongsanpo Jisaepo Saryang Dangpo Jorapo Angolpo Mijohang Sobipo Gadeok Cheonseongpo Yulpo

In 1457, the Joseon military was reorganized along the *Jin-gwan* garrison system, optimal for provincial defence and dealing with rebellions, but, in the 1500s, it proved to be ineffective for concentrating troops against new threats by the Jurchens in the north and Wako pirates in the south. In the 1550s, the Joseon military was reformed under the *Jeseungbangryak* system. Under this model, coastal counties and their magistrates were also placed under the authority of a *Jeoldosa* (fleet commander/admiral). In anticipation of the Japanese invasion, the Joseon military had shuffled its most aggressive and hard-fighting officers to the southern navies in the year prior to the invasion.

Land administrative districts	
Gyeongsang Right Navy	Ulsan, Gijang
Gyeongsang Left Navy	Ungcheon, Jinhae, Goseong, Geoje, Sacheon, Namhae, Gonyang, Hadong
Jeolla Left Navy	Suncheon, Boseong, Nakan, Heungyang, Gwangyang
Jeolla Right Navy	Jangheung, Najoo, Heungdeok, Gangjin, Muan, Gobu, Haenam, Hampyeong, Buan, Yeongam, Yeonggwang, Okgu, Jindo, Mujang

Commanders

Yi Sun-sin (8d 3m 1545–19d 11m 1598, Deoksu Yi clan) was born the third son of provincial yangban Yi Jeong and Lady Byeon. He had been born in the Joseon capital of Hanyang, near a military base, so as a result, reportedly played soldier with his friends in his youth, building fortifications by the road and the like (as this book's author once did, and his father before him). Ironically, the future Chief State Councillor and Yi's patron and friend Ryu Seong-ryong also lived in the same neighbourhood, as did Won Gyun, Yi's future subordinate. Yi's family moved to Asan, where Yi spent his teenage years. At age 21, he married Lady Bang, the daughter of Boseong magistrate Bang Jin. In all, he had eight children, three sons and one daughter with Lady Bang and two sons and two daughters with his concubine Lady Oh. Perhaps influenced by his father-in-law, Yi took the military service exam in the eighth lunar month of 1572 at age 28, but failed to pass when he fell from his horse and broke his left leg. Yi trained and studied for four years, finally passing in the second lunar month of 1576, scoring 12th in his cohort. Yi's record until the Imjin War is a fascinating example of a typical career officer's life, with all its ups and downs.

Yi Sun-sin's military career prior to the Imjin War

1576 (12m)	*Dongbubu Gwungwan* (9th rank) in Hamgyong Province
1579 (2m)	8th rank officer at the Hansung training centre
1579 (10m)	Transferred to the Haemi military camp in Chungcheondo
1580 (7m)	Goheung Balpo *Manho* (4th rank) in the Jeolla Left Navy
1582 (1m)	Dismissed after a false accusation of dereliction of duty
1582 (5m)	Reinstated as an 8th rank training centre officer
1583 (7m)	Assigned to South Hamgyong as a *Geonwonbo Gwongwan* (8th rank)
1583 (10m)	Promoted to *Geonwonbo Chamgun* (7th rank)
1584–85	Leaves post to enter a mourning period after his father's death in 11m 1583
1586 (1m)	*Sabuksi Jubu* (6th rank)
1586 (2m)	Josanbo *Manho* (4th rank)
1587 (8m)	Concurrently held the position of Nokdundo Island garrison commander

1587 (10m)		Court-martialled by General Yi Il after the battle of Nokdundo against the Jurchens
1588 (1m)		Receives an honourable discharge after further combat against the Jurchens
1589 (2m)		Re-recruited and appointed *Jobangjang* (chief of staff) to the governor of Jeolla
1589 (12m)		Promoted to Magistrate (4th rank) of Jeongeup, Jeolla Province, at the recommendation of childhood friend Ryu Seong-ryong; concurrently served as the Magistrate of Taein County (6th rank)
1591 (2m)		Promoted to Jeolla Left Navy Jeoldosa

Yi's career prior to the Imjin War was largely peaceful other than a brief stint fighting the Jurchen tribes in the north. His most notable action was as garrison commander of Nokdundo Island (located today in Russia). Nokdundo had a population of 800, mostly farmers, protected by a small garrison of a few dozen soldiers and a palisade fort. In the eighth lunar month of 1587, some 100 Jurchens attacked Nokdundo. While Yi and his men fought courageously, even killing the Jurchen leader, they were badly outnumbered and lost ten men killed and 160 civilians and 15 horses captured. Yi pursued the raiders, killing three Jurchens and rescuing 60 civilians. In spite of his efforts, his higher-ups saw a defeat as a defeat, refusing to consider the details, and had him court-martialled. Yi was given a *Baekui Jonggun*, whereby he was stripped of his rank but given an opportunity to redeem himself on the battlefield. In the first lunar month of 1588, Yi participated in an attack on the Jurchen village of Shijeon with 2,500 troops, rescuing countless captives and livestock, killing dozens of Jurchens and burning down about 200 homes.

When Yi took up his appointment as Jeoldosa of the Jeolla Left Navy, his only prior naval experience was a brief stint as the *Manho* (port captain) of Goheung and Josanbo. Yi devoted himself to his new post, delving into intensive study to master his profession. His friend Ryu Seong-ryong sent him a military treatise he had authored, a book that Yi read cover to cover to take its lessons to heart. The brief time between Yi's appointment and the war was a fruitful period for the Jeolla Left Navy. A disciplinarian, he worked hard to turn his gaggle of conscripts into a respectable navy that would be able to fight when the rumoured Japanese invasion occurred through constant drills and exercises.

Yi won a string of victories in the early years of the Imjin War. But in 1597, Yi was arrested, tortured and sacked after refusing to carry out an offensive ordered on unreliable intelligence. After the Joseon navy was annihilated at the battle of Chilcheollyang, Yi was reinstated. He found his finest hour at Myeongyang, where he led the navy's 13 surviving ships to an impossible victory against a Japanese fleet of 300. Yi carefully rebuilt the Joseon navy once more to its former glory, and fought without rest to push the Japanese

A 1978 portrait by Jeong Hyeong-mo imagining what Admiral Yi may have looked like. Most modern portraits such as this one portray him as a wise and kindly looking man. Go Sang-a, a magistrate who spent two weeks with Yi in 1594 to supervise military examinations, left the most detailed account of Yi's appearance, writing, 'His eloquence and wisdom were truly capable of calming unrest. However, his face was sallow and his lips shrunken.' Go, who dabbled in physiognomy and fortune telling, thought Yi's features to be inauspicious. More realistically Yi's exhausted appearance was a symptom of the fevers the overworked admiral was experiencing at the time of Go's visit, something that Go seemed to have been unaware of. Yi made a great effort to appear well before his guests and carry out normal duties, only confiding his condition to his family and senior officers. (Courtesy of the Jeseungdang)

The tomb of Admiral Yi in Asan, South Korea. Yi is buried here with his wife, Lady Bang. He was originally buried elsewhere in Asan after his death at the 1598 battle of Noryang, but the tomb was moved to its present location in 1614 after King Gwanghaegun honoured Yi for his services posthumously. (Photograph by Jeon Hyeong-jun, Korea Tourism Organization)

out of their strongholds on the Korean coast. Like Nelson at Trafalgar, he was killed at the battle of Noryang on the eve of victory, inflicting one final defeat on the Japanese fleet as it fled from Korea at last.

Yi is today revered in Korea, both North and South. His historical legacy has been the subject of much revision for socio-political purposes in the late Joseon, postcolonial and dictatorship eras. Those in power have exaggerated certain character traits over time, to turn him into a superhuman symbol of resistance, loyalty or patriotism. Nonetheless, such exaggerations did emerge from reality, and from the primary sources it is possible to glimpse the man behind the myth.

Yi's diary, the *Nanjung Ilgi*, reveals his humanity. It is clear that he was a man under immense exhaustion and stress, who took the burden of command and war personally. He records his emotions and thoughts freely as any modern diary writer does, and at times skips entries on what must have been particularly busy days. His dislike of Won Gyun is mentioned frequently, as are his feelings of loss and frustration when faced with bureaucratic roadblocks or logistical nightmares, as well as his anger when hearing of Japanese atrocities. Yi was humble and self-effacing, and his desire to do his utmost, combined with his frequent feelings of frustration and helplessness, led him to be overly hard on himself at times. Above all, he was someone who cared deeply about his family. He writes of his happiness when his children visited him at his headquarters, and when he heard via messenger ship how his mother was doing. When the magistrate of Goseong sent him beef skewers, medicine and a jar of honey, Yi writes that in spite of being ill that day, 'I felt bad about accepting it because it was a funerary period [his aunt had passed away the day before], but it

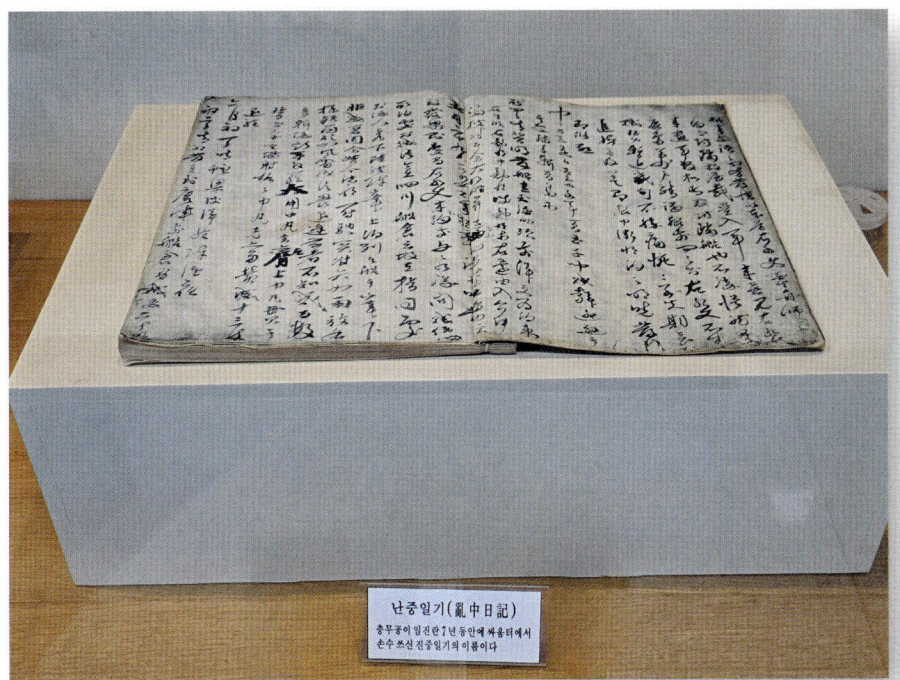

A copy of the *Nanjung Ilgi*. Yi's diary is registered as part of the UNESCO Memory of the World for its cultural and historical significance. Written in a daily format, the diary records the highlights of Yi's day, going on at length if there was a battle, but at other times simply noting the weather. Yi's official battle reports seem to have been derived from what he writes in his diary, with occasional differences in details. (Photograph by Kim Min-su, Okpo Battle Memorial Park)

was a gift that had been given with so much consideration and could not be sent back, so I gave it to my officers.'

He also demonstrated a deep personal concern for the welfare of ordinary citizens of Joseon Korea in a stratified society during a time of great suffering, often considering in his battle plans whether the Joseon navy was pushing the Japanese to retreat into Joseon civilians. Yi declared in one report, 'To find our people who had been carried away by the enemy and to recapture them alive is a merit equal to beheading the enemy robbers.' He gave his captains explicit orders to search carefully for Joseon prisoners on the Japanese ships they boarded, and made note of who rescued how many in his reports, essentially equating rescuing a civilian to killing an enemy. Though the strategic impact of Yi's 1592 campaigns has been somewhat embellished over time, his engagements demonstrate that he was nonetheless a first-rate military commander who achieved victories against formidable opponents. Yi was a man of admirable moral character. He carried out his service with dignity and skill, driven by an unbreakable sense of duty to his king and country. This sentiment he carried all throughout his career is reflected in his posthumous title: *Chungmugong*, meaning 'Lord of Loyal Valor'. Yi is a national hero in South Korea, and a 17m statue of him stands in Gwanghwamun Plaza in the heart of Seoul, kept in good company by a statue of King Sejong, the creator of the Korean language.

The Yi Sun-sin statue at Gwanghwamun Plaza is one of Seoul's landmark features. The geobukseon display before it is a recent addition. (Photograph by Yuhan Kim)

A modern portrait of Yi Eok-gi at the Chungminsa shrine in Yeosu, where he is enshrined. (From the Chungminsa shrine)

Yi Eok-gi (3d 9m 1561–15d 9m 1597), of the Jeonju Lee (Yi) clan, served alongside Yi Sun-sin as commander of the Jeolla Right Navy. Yi Eok-gi showed an aptitude for military affairs from an early age, passing the military service examination in his teens, and was appointed *Dohobu* (provincial magistrate) of Gyeongheung at the age of just 21. Like Yi Sun-sin, his first taste of combat was in the north against the Jurchens, defeating a raiding tribe. At 26, he was appointed magistrate of the frontier district of Onseong in the northern Hamgyong Province, coincidentally where Yi Sun-sin was also stationed. At 32, he was transferred all the way south to be commander of the Suncheon garrison and promoted to command the Jeolla Right Navy in 1592. Go Sang-a was critical of Yi Eok-gi, writing, 'Yi Eok-gi was restless so lacked substantive inner virtue and thus seemed lost.' While he was much belated in joining Yi in 1592, Yi Eok-gi was a competent enough commander and vouched for Yi Sun-sin when the latter was arrested and dismissed in 1597. He was killed at the battle of Chilcheollyang, along with most of the Joseon navy. Today, Submarine SS-071 of the Republic of Korea (ROK) Navy is named after him.

Won Gyun (5d 1m 1540–15d 7m 1597) was born into a military family and passed the military exam at age 28, serving in various magistrate positions and fighting the Jurchens. In 1592, on the eve of war, he was appointed as Jeoldosa of the Gyeongsang Right Navy. His service under Yi was marred with mutual dislike due to Won's inaccurate reports to court, perceived incompetence and insubordination. He was known to be a heavy drinker, at times to Yi's disgust, but in his diary entry for 26d 8m 1593, Yi writes, 'While serving ancestral rite food, Won Gyun said he wanted to drink so I gave him some, and he got really drunk and started talking nonsense. It was funny.' A slanderous feud emerged between the two men in 1594, contributing to Yi's removal and arrest in 1597 after King Seonjo sided with Won. Appointed to Yi's position as *Samdosugun Tongjesa* (Naval Commander of the Three Provinces) after Yi's removal, he found himself completely out of his depth and led the armada that Yi had so carefully built up to destruction at the battle of Chilcheollyang, where he was killed. His posthumous legacy was the subject of much controversy, with King Seonjo facing backlash for seeking to honour someone who had given so much headache to Yi and who was responsible for almost single-handedly turning the war in favour of the Japanese in 1597. Go noted, 'Won Gyun was rough and fierce, but lacked wisdom and also did not win the hearts of the people,' indicating he was an aggressive fighter, but lacked leadership, organizational aptitude and tact. Won Gyun's disparagement of Yi in his official reports makes him the most controversial figure in the Imjin War.

Captains
Like Nelson, Yi had his own 'band of brothers' and enjoyed a close relationship with his subordinates. It was more than just an amicable mentor–mentee or

superior–subordinate relationship; Yi and his captains were friends in the truest sense. They celebrated one another's birthdays, dined and drank with each other, played Baduk (Go) or Jjangi (chess), practised archery and spent long hours into the night in deep discussion, finding comfort in camaraderie during a time when their country was plunged into blood and darkness.

Jeolla Left Navy Command

Rank	Name
Bangdap Cheomsa	Yi Sun-sin (M)
Nakan County Magistrate	Shin Ho
Heungyang Country Magistrate	Bae Hong-rip
Gwangyang County Magistrate	Eo Yeong-dam
Balpo Training Officer	Na Dae-yong
Boseong County Magistrate	Kim Deuk-gwang
Nokdo Manho	Jeong Un
Yeodo Gwun-gwan (9th rank)	Kim In-young
Sado Cheomsa	Kim Wan
Jeolla Left Navy HQ Officer	Choi Dae-sung
Jeolla Left Navy HQ Officer	Bae Eung-rok
Jeolla Left Navy HQ Officer	Lee Eon-ryang

Kwon Jun (1547–1611, Andong Kwon clan) was married to Jo Hwi-won, the younger sister of Field Marshal Kwon Yul's wife. He passed the military exam in 1579 and was serving as magistrate of Suncheon at the outbreak of war. Suncheon was the largest of the counties under the jurisdiction of the Jeolla Left Navy. As such, he served as Yi's second-in-command. He resigned after Yi's ousting and Won Gyun's appointment as commander of the combined Joseon fleet. When Yi was reinstated, Kwon was appointed naval commander of Chungcheong Province, but saw little combat.

The archery range at the Jeseungdang, where Yi and his officers would have practised their marksmanship. (Photograph by Lee Beom-su, Korea Tourism Organization)

A helmet and quiver as ornately decorated as these could only have belonged to members of the royal family or high-ranking generals. Regional fleet commanders would have worn something less resplendent than this, though still more decorated than the armour of most Joseon troops. (From the collection of the National Museum of Korea, accessible at https://www.emuseum.go.kr/)

Kwon was one of Yi's closest friends, and the admiral often spent his free time with Kwon and his brothers.

Eo Yeong-dam (1534–94) passed the military examination in 1564 and was serving as the magistrate of Gwangyang County at the outbreak of war. Having served as a garrison commander in the Jinhae region, he brought considerable knowledge of the local coastline to campaign planning meetings. Yi also considered him to be an excellent tactician. Much to Yi's sorrow, he died of disease on 9d 4m 1594.

Yi Sun-sin (Muui-gong; M) (27d 11m 1554–1d 9m 1611) had the same name as his commander (albeit with different Chinese characters) but was from a different Yi clan, the Jeonju Yi. He is typically distinguished from his commander via his posthumous title, Muui-gong. Yi (M) passed the military exam in 1578, serving in various magisterial positions, though he had been dismissed twice before being appointed as Cheomsa of Bangdap in 1591 as part of the Joseon military's manpower shift in response to rumors of a Japanese invasion.

Yi (M)'s spotty peacetime record belied an aggressive and active commander, who soon earned a reputation as one of the Jeolla Left Navy's best officers. When Yi (M) was excluded from the rewards and citations from the royal court in the wake of the 1592 operations, Yi wrote a detailed report on Yi's (M) actions in the campaigns, noting that the omission puzzled everyone and that 'I hope that the King's Court will send down orders to bestow rewards on him,' which was duly done. After the war, Yi (M) continued his military service until his death, becoming a commander in the guards. The two Yis were close friends. Submarine SS-068 of the ROK Navy is named after him.

Jeong Un (1543–92) passed the military exam in 1570, moving up the ranks as Yi did to eventually become magistrate of Jeju Island. However, his

A drawing of Jeong Un, at the Chungmusa shrine in Suncheon where he and other Joseon officers are enshrined. His death at the battle of Busan was greatly mourned by Yi, who considered him his right-hand man and among his best officers for his aggressive spirit in battle. (From the Suncheon Tourism Association)

incorruptible personality often put him in conflict with his superiors, resulting in his dismissal. In 1591, he was appointed Manho of Nokdo Island. Jeong Un kept his ships well prepared for war, and was a skilled and aggressive commander. Yi wrote of Jeong Un, 'He was one of the few staff officers on whom I placed complete confidence. In the three major victories he always stood at the forefront. At the battle of Busan, in particular, he plunged into peril, braving death, thrusting into the enemy positions, raining projectiles the whole day, and keeping the trembling Japanese at bay.' Submarine SS-067 of the ROK Navy is named after him.

Na Dae-yong (1556–1612) was originally a teacher at a Confucian school and passed the military examination in 1583. He served most prominently as one of the Jeolla Left Navy's chief shipbuilders, responsible for the construction of the geobukseon. After the war, he continued to work as an engineer in the Joseon navy, improving existing vessels and developing new ones. In 1611, he was appointed Jeoldosa of the Gyeonggi Province Navy, but suffering from his injuries from the war, died the next year. Submarine SS-069 of the ROK Navy is named after him.

JAPANESE

Commanders

The men of the Joseon navy were career officers trudging their way up and down an institutionalized military, promotions determined largely by who they knew and what postings opened up. In contrast, the Japanese naval commanders were self-made leaders whose careers swung on personal feats of glory in a country where such opportunities abounded. If the Joseon military structure allowed for men such as Won Gyun to climb far above their abilities to positions of high command, there was no such room for weakness in the high ranks of Hideyoshi's armies. The violence of the Sengoku wars had filtered out the weak, incompetent and unlucky, leaving only battle-hardened professionals born from decades of violence. No commander that Hideyoshi sent into Korea could be called incompetent or a poor soldier. In spite of countless disastrous defeats at the hands of Yi, much to their credit, they stretched their resources and improvised to, if not win, survive the attacks of the Joseon fleet.

Wakizaka Yasuharu (1554–1626) was originally a vassal of Oda Nobunaga, but transferred to become a retainer of Hideyoshi sometime in the late 1570s. He distinguished himself in the battle of Mikijozeme in 1580 and was rewarded with a Horo cloak decorated with a white ring, which would become the origin of the white rings on his family crest. He achieved fame at the battle of Shizugatake (1583), becoming known as one of the 'Seven Spears of Shizugatake', the seven Hideyoshi retainers who distinguished themselves in the battle. In the next few years, his efforts in battle earned him 10,000 *koku* (an area of land used in wealth measurement, each equivalent to 150kg of rice production) in Settsu Province, 20,000 in Yamato Province and 30,000 in Awaji. In 1587, he was appointed commander of Toyotomi Hideyoshi's navy and led it in the Kyushu campaign against the Shimazu clan, as well as the Odawara campaign.

Wakizaka originally joined the invasion of Korea as a ground commander, earning what was perhaps his greatest victory in that war.

A woodblock print of Wakizaka Yasuharu by Asakaro Hoiki, as he appears in the 1867 edition of *Tales of Heroes from the Taiheiki*, a collection of stories about samurai and their heroics. The book was famous for its characterizing illustrations that captured the essential characteristics of each samurai – here Wakizaka is depicted in a ferocious manner, a far cry from the bureaucratic-looking figure in his official portrait. (From the Tokyo Metropolitan Library)

In 6m 1592, Governor Yi Kwang marched out of Jeolla Province with an army 50,000–80,000 strong to liberate Hanyang. A Korean vanguard of 2,000 men attacked 600 men under Wakizaka's subordinate Watanabe Shichiemon at Bukdumunsan mountain on 4d 6m. Watanabe fell back to Munsosan mountain, where he held out, awaiting Wakizaka's reinforcements from Hanyang. Wakizaka arrived the next day at noon with 1,000 men. He struck the Joseon right flank while Watanabe sallied out of the fort to attack from the front, and the exhausted Joseon vanguard was routed. Yi Kwang fell back to reorganize his demoralized army, but encamped it on flat ground instead of defensible high ground. Despite being terribly outnumbered, Wakizaka charged the Joseon army the next morning, catching his enemy eating breakfast. His ferocious shock attack captured many ranking Joseon officers and the leaderless army disintegrated, abandoning weapons and equipment as they fled back south. Given his experience thus far in the war, Wakizaka did not have a high opinion of Joseon's military forces, a belief that undoubtedly played a role in his decision-making at Hansando. In spite of his defeat at the hands of Yi, Wakizaka was undoubtedly a skilled commander who quickly learned from experience.

After the Imjin War, Wakizaka flip-flopped around in the turbulent war of succession in the wake of Hideyoshi's death. He originally planned to side with Tokugawa Ieyasu, but joined Ishida Mitsunari at the battle of Sekigahara in 1600, only to defect back to the Tokugawa side. After Todo Takatora, his old comrade from the Imjin War, threw in a good word for him with Tokugawa, Wakizaka was not punished for siding with Ishida at the start. He was instead given the Ozu Domain. He retired in 1615 to become a monk, the most peaceful end of any of the protagonists in this book.

A portrait of Kuki Yoshitaka. Kuki's astute reporting on Joseon tactics formed the basis for the overhauls in the Japanese strategy to counter Yi. (Courtesy of the Joan-ji Temple, Toba City)

Kuki Yoshitaka (1542–1600) was the preeminent naval commander of the Sengoku era and among the most able of Yi's opponents. At Angolpo, in the face of overwhelming firepower, he demonstrated remarkable resilience and command ability, saving the flagship *Nihon Maru*. The Kuki clan was from the Shima Province and operated as pirates (indeed, Yoshitaka's father Kuki Sadakata was one). Kuki took his family name to legitimacy and power after pledging fealty to Oda Nobunaga in 1569 and commanding the Nobunaga fleet in the campaigns against the Ikko-Ikki. At the third siege of Nagashino, Kuki's fleet supported ground troops to victory by bombarding the Ikko-Ikki position and blockading the fortress. During the 11-year siege of Ishiyama-Honganji, Kuki blockaded the fortress in 1576 with a fleet of 300 ships. However, at the battle of Kizugawaguchi, Mori Terumoto's 700 ships defeated Kuki's fleet and broke through the blockade. Undeterred, Kuki built a flotilla of six cannon-armed *atakebune* and used it to defeat the Mori navy at the second battle of Kizugawaguchi. In 1582, Kuki threw his lot in with Toyotomi Hideyoshi and was given Toba Castle. Kuki led his fleet in Hideyoshi's campaigns to consolidate power over Japan, notably in the Kyushu campaign.

Kuki met a tragic end, for like so many of his comrades who participated in the Imjin War, Kuki fought at Sekigahara – but for the losing side. It was worse for Kuki, as his son, Kuki Moritaka, was on the other side of the battlefield fighting for Tokugawa Ieyasu. This ironically allowed Kuki Moritaka to intervene on his father's behalf when the moment of *vae victis* arrived, but in Shakespearean fashion, the message that he had been spared reached Kuki too late, after he had committed *seppuku*.

Kato Yoshiaki (1563–1631) was born in Mikawa and had a childhood of unfortunate events. The year Kato was born, his father, Kato Noriaki, joined an Ikko-Ikki revolt against Matsudaira Ieyasu despite being a vassal of the latter. When the rebellion was crushed, the Kato family fled, wandering homeless under a false name. They entered into the service of Toyotomi Hideyoshi, where Kato became a page for Hideyoshi's adopted son Hashiba

A statue of Kato Yoshiaki in Matsuyama. The statue is sculpted after the armour Kato wore at Sekigahara. Matsuyama Castle was awarded to Kato after Sekigahara, but he was transferred to Aizu before he finished its construction. (Courtesy of Kees van Tilburg, https://equestrianstatue.org/)

Hidekatsu. As the story goes, in 1576, Kato snuck into the army without permission. Hashiba's mother asked Hideyoshi to punish the young Kato and expel him from the army, but Hideyoshi laughed and gave the young Kato an official soldier's salary. His trust was to be well rewarded. In Kato's first action, at the 1578 battle of Miki, he took the heads of two enemy soldiers – despite being only 15 years old. Like Wakizaka, he also fought at Shizugatake and was one of the 'Seven Spears'. Continued service enriched him, ultimately earning him the rank of daimyo, 15,000 koku in Awaji and lordship of Shichi Castle in 1585. He led a naval force in the Kyushu campaign and the siege of Odawara.

After the Imjin War, Kato sided with Tokugawa Ieyasu, fighting at Sekigahara. Ieyasu generously rewarded his allies, and Kato walked away with 200,000 koku in Iyo Province, where he built his stronghold, Matsuyama Castle, in 1601. He became something of a builder, partaking in the construction of numerous castles around Japan. This constructive streak did not last long, as Kato took to the field one last time in the great siege of Osaka against the remnants of the Toyotomi clan, finishing off the legacy of his old master. He served as a senior official to the Tokugawa Shogunate and died in 1631 after an illness.

Todo Takatora (1556–1630) was born to a samurai family, which had fallen on hard times and lived as farmers on the land they used to rule. Like Hideyoshi, Todo began his military career as a lowly ashigaru. He had his first taste of combat at age 14, serving alongside his father at the battle of Anegawa, where he took a head. He hopped around the armies of various lords, living paycheque to paycheque and often leaving restaurants without paying. In 1576, he joined the army of Toyotomi Hidenaga (Hideyoshi's younger brother), his fifth lord in three years. He distinguished himself in combat and found his life's calling in castle design and construction, and a reputation for professionalism soon followed. Appointed to build a castle for Tokugawa Ieyasu in 1586, Todo

A statue of Todo Takatora stands at the foot of Imabari Castle. Todo was awarded the Imabari domain after Sekigahara, and constructed the massive castle in 1608. Todo had just a year to enjoy his new home as in 1609 he was transferred to another fief in line with the Shogunate's policy of moving around their daimyos to minimize their regional ties to reduce the possibility of rebellion. Imabari was given to Todo's adopted son. (Courtesy of Kees van Tilburg, https://equestrianstatue.org/)

took one look at the blueprint given to him and scrapped it due to its perceived weak points. He heavily edited the design, and even paid out of his own pocket for the additions for a more complete castle – the touch of only someone with confidence and pride in their craft. This left a deep impression on Ieyasu and began a friendship that would last a lifetime (and beyond).

Todo was left unemployed when Toyotomi Hidenaga died, and sought an early retirement as a monk in 1595. However, Toyotomi Hideyoshi put an end to such plans, granting him a fiefdom of 70,000 koku in Iyo Province and sending him back to Korea. When it came time to choose sides for the coming storm at Sekigahara, Todo must have been torn – whether to serve the family that had taken him on as a lowly ashigaru and given him the road to fame (as Napoleon said of Marshal Lannes, 'I found him a pygmy and left him a giant') or to aid Tokugawa Ieyasu, who was by now one of Todo's closest friends. Todo chose the latter, and reportedly played a key role in enticing Wakizaka Yasuharu and several other key daimyos to defect on the eve of the battle of Sekigahara. Todo reaped the fruits of victory, being granted 120,000 koku in Iyo Province, and, naturally, went back to castle building. The Vauban of Japan, Todo designed and built some 20 castles throughout his lifetime. He was at the deathbed of his old friend Ieyasu when the latter asked Todo to build his mausoleum – the Ueno Toshogu Shrine. Todo, who had jumped from one lord to another throughout his life, in turn pledged his friend his loyalty in the next life.

OPPOSING FORCES

The Joseon and Japanese navies could not have been more asymmetric in purpose, tactical doctrine and design. In a sense, they almost complemented each other. However, the fundamental difference between the fleets in the 1592 campaign was that the Japanese ships were transports, while the Joseon ships were purpose-built warships – a contrast that was clear when both fleets were put to the test in battle. This near-perfect asymmetry can be explained by a relative lack of knowledge among the Joseon and Japanese leadership of each other's military capabilities. Indeed, the Joseon court entered the war thinking that the Japanese were weak on land and strong on water. Intelligence regarding the naval tactics and technology of the enemy appears to have hardly made its way into the strategic planning of either side prior to the war.

JOSEON

At the time of the Imjin War, the Joseon navy was organized into provincial fleets. The most combat-ready were the ones in Chungcheong, Gyeongsang and Jeolla provinces, as these were the ones that dealt with Japanese pirates the most – fleets in five provinces tended to be no more than coastguard units. It was one of the battle fleets, the Jeolla Left Navy, that Yi commanded as a *Sugeun Jeoldosa* (regional fleet admiral).

In 1458, the Joseon dynasty reorganized its military system. The threats from the Jurchens had subsided and the Wako pirates had been suppressed. The new Jin-gwan system was designed to fight local wars and small-scale

The barrel of a *Cheonja chongtong*, made in 1555. Joseon artillery nomenclature was based off the 'Thousand Character Classic', with Cheonja meaning 'heaven', the first character in the textbook. Cannon of lower calibres took after subsequent characters, equivalent to classifying cannons as 'A, B, C…' The barrel was affixed to a wooden carriage by ropes bound through two moulded handles, which have since broken off in this particular example. (From the collection of the National Museum of Korea, accessible at https://www.emuseum.go.kr/)

incursions rather than a full invasion. Each province had its own land and naval forces, and governors doubled in function as military commanders.

In the decades preceding the Japanese invasion, Joseon's naval forces had been greatly strengthened in response to clashes with Japanese pirates. The Jeolla Left Navy in particular was kept in a state of readiness, after a Joseon naval defeat at the battle of Sojukdo Island in 1587.

In the year and two months between his appointment and the Japanese invasion, Yi had made immense progress in bolstering the military capabilities of his command. He constructed a fortress near Yeosu to protect the naval base there from landward attacks, installed a metal chain between Dolsan Island and the mainland to block the coastal approach to Yeosu and began work on the geobukseon, his signature assault ship. Artillery and munitions were well stocked, and Yi was fortunate to have under him competent subordinates who spearheaded the expansion of the fleet. Yi was acutely aware of the threat posed by Japanese land forces and, in addition to fortifying his naval bases, he attempted to procure some cavalry. Indeed, the prospect of amphibious or joint land–sea operations was never far from his mind.

The Joseon navy primarily relied on firepower tactics, driven by an impressive artillery arsenal. Joseon cannons (*chongtong*) were divided into four calibres. Typically made of copper alloy, the cannons were capable of firing large arrow missiles, solid shot or iron bullets and pebbles as grapeshot.

Joseon artillery

Cannon	Calibre	Maximum Range	Ammunition
Cheonja chongtong (cannon)	12.8cm	1.4km	Used the *daejanggunjeon* (arrow missile of 247.5cm) or 400 grapeshot. The Cheonja chongtong was also known to fire a lead-coated cannonball and 100 grapeshot together. Each *panokseon* (standard Joseon warship) had one or two of these heavy guns mounted on the front. The daejanggunjeon was not used often, as each shot consumed over a kilogram of gunpowder.
Jija chongtong	10.3cm	1km	Used the *janggunjeon* (192cm) or 200 grapeshot
Hyeonja chongtong	6.5cm	700m	Used the *chadaejeon* (132.5cm) or 100 grapeshot
Hwangja chongtong	4cm	300m	Used the *piryongchajungjeon* (131cm) or 40 grapeshot

The Hyeonja chongtong was the most common shipboard artillery, and for good reason. Each shot used up just four *nyang* (160g) of gunpowder. This particular cannon was made from copper alloy in 1596 and discovered in 1985 in Gohyeon bay. (From the collection of the Jinju National Museum, accessible at https://www.emuseum.go.kr/)

The jungwangu was a medium Joseon mortar. This particular one was cast in 1590. (From the collection of the Jinju National Museum, accessible at https://www.emuseum.go.kr/)

The Joseon navy was also equipped with wide-mouthed mortars (*daewangu*, large calibre and *jungwangu*, medium calibre) that were used to bombard coastal positions or hurl *bigyeokjincheonroe* onto enemy ships. The bigyeokjincheonroe was a timed-fuse bomb filled with triangular metal shards that would explode with a fragmentation effect. Another weapon used was the *hwacha*, a wooden frame that fired 100 *shingijeon*, rocket-propelled explosive arrows, to an effective range of around 200m, but a maximum range of 1,000m.

The shingijeon hwacha was a rocket-launcher frame developed in the 1400s. The hwacha could simultaneously fire up to 100 shingijeon arrows with an explosive self-propellant that often had a double charge that would explode after hitting the target. Hwacha refers to the frame, and shingijeon refers to the propelled arrow. (From the collection of the Jinju National Museum, accessible at https://www.emuseum.go.kr/)

The *chongtonggi hwacha* (also known as the *hwa-go*) was a variant of the hwacha developed in 1451. It was a volley gun with 50 *sajeonchongtong* (early Joseon cannon) barrels that could fire a cluster of four to six flechettes. The barrels were fired ten at a time, by rows. (From the collection of the Jinju National Museum, accessible at https://www.emuseum.go.kr/)

Joseon marines and sailors conducted small-arms combat with bows and arrows, or the *Seungja chongtong*, a hand cannon. Joseon troops had found these to be effective against the Jurchens, and it had a range of around 200m. In spite of the impressive ordnance of Joseon warships, the Joseon army had not adopted arquebuses as the Japanese had.

Most Jeolla Left Navy personnel were recruited locally and thus familiar with the water. Not all were regular navy men – the Righteous Army guerrillas that became prominent in the Imjin War even took on a naval form, as Yi notes of one 'Cho Chong, horse farm supervisor of

This particular Seungja chongtong was made by the craftsman Gyu-ga in 1579. Ironically, the Seungja chongtong was first designed in 1575 by Yi Sun-sin's predecessor, Jeolla Left Naval Jeoldosa Kim Ji. The back had a hole that was affixed to a wooden pole. It was a shotgun that could shoot a variety of projectiles from a cluster of 15 anti-personnel buckshot to armour-piercing flechettes (*piryeong-mokjeon*), using just 1 nyang (37g) of gunpowder. While effective against the Jurchens, it was found to be out-ranged by the Japanese arquebus and phased out as the main infantry firearm after the Imjin War in favour of the matchlock. (From the collection of the National Museum of Korea, accessible at https://www.emuseum.go.kr/)

Joseon armour. Usually only officers or elite troops would have worn quality armour. This particular one, dated to the 17th century, is a dujeonggap brigandine-style armour. Iron or leather scales (in this case the latter) were attached to the fabric by iron studs. While Joseon troops used a wide variety of armour in the Imjin War including lamellar and chainmail, by the late Joseon era, the dujeonggap had become the most popular, becoming emblematic of the Joseon military. (From the collection of the National Museum of Korea, accessible at https://www.emuseum.go.kr/)

Suncheon, who fitted out a boat with his own funds and participated in the battle [of Busan] with his slaves and cowherds as volunteers, killing many Japanese and taking many spoils of war, as repeatedly reported by Kwon Jun, the Center Forward Leader.' Another guerrilla, Song Oong-chi, noted to be a 'hermit of Suncheon', formed his own Righteous Army and Yi tasked his band with forming the Suncheon city garrison, and even provided him with a panokseon to give his group naval capabilities. Most of Yi's sailors were conscripted slaves, farmers or fishermen, however, and needed to be at home some of the time to plant and harvest. This was absolutely necessary because the army and navy also depended on this harvest for food. Desertion was always a problem that Yi had to address, especially given that Yi's homesick men were fighting close to their homes. Victories and glory alone were not enough to keep the conscript sailors at their posts, and Yi had his men sleep on their ships at night when on campaign, both for fear of a Japanese attack from land and to make desertion more difficult.

The standard warship of the Joseon kingdom was the panokseon, a three-level ship some 70–100ft in length, with 14–18 guns, and 8–10 oars on each side. The panokseon was a very sturdy ship, typically built with pine and using wooden pegs in lieu of nails. While not designed for lengthy ocean travel, it was excellent for its intended use – coastal defence in the rough waters of southern Korea. The ship was, in many ways, designed to be a floating artillery battery. It had a flat-bottomed U-shaped hull that made it slow by providing greater resistance against currents, but that same feature made the ship manoeuvrable and enabled it to rotate easily on rough waters to present its broadsides. The bottom level housed supplies and ballast, the middle deck the oarsmen and the open upper deck was the main combat platform with the artillery and a command pavilion. A panokseon crew consisted of around 160 men, though in 12m 1592, Yi reported that he needed a minimum of 130 men for a panokseon to be combat effective. A panokseon typically had eight specialists: two each of *ta-gong* (rudder), *yo-su* (sails), *bu-sang* (navigation) and *jeong-su* (anchor). There were around 100 oarsmen, with four oarsmen and one leader per oar, and a reserve of 20 men such that the oars were operated on a rotational shift system to minimize exhaustion. In desperate situations, the oarsmen could

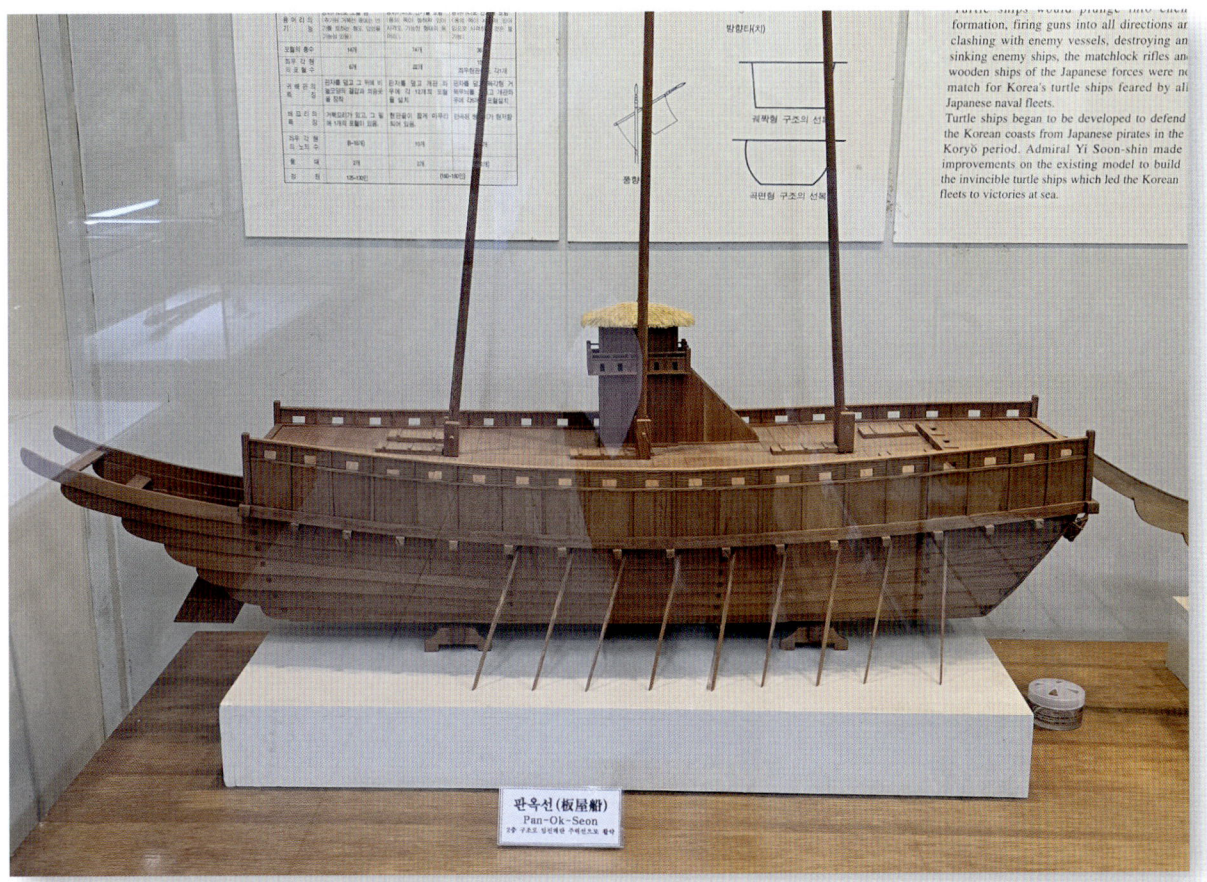

The panokseon was the workhorse of the Joseon navy and Yi's effective use of its strengths was critical to his victories. Before the panokseon was adopted, the *maengseon* was the mainstay of the Joseon navy, but it was a dual-use civilian transport ship that could mount cannons. The panokseon, in contrast, was a dedicated warship that emerged from the threat posed by Chinese and Japanese pirates. (Photograph by Kim Min-su, Okpo Battle Memorial Park)

double as combat troops, but it does not appear that they were normally intended to do so. The proportions within the combat contingent fluctuated, but there were probably around 15–18 archers, ten gunpowder weapons specialists and 24 artillerymen. The low complement of naval artillerymen indicates that only a portion of the guns would have been manned at one time, consistent with the stable design of the panokseon to easily change facing and present a pre-loaded side after a broadside from the other.

Among the most fascinating aspects of the Imjin War was the geobukseon, a powerful assault ship known as the 'turtle ship'. At the time these ships were called 'gwiseon' (an older way of saying turtle ship), but the term 'geobukseon' has emerged to encompass all Joseon ships of this type. Yi had this ship specially built in preparation for the rumoured Japanese invasion, designed as a shock assault ship that would break up enemy formations by charging into them and firing at close range, and also launching decapitation strikes by targeting enemy flagships. At the start of the Imjin War, there were three geobukseon under construction: *Yeonggwiseon* (captained by Lee Gi-nam), in the Jeolla Left Navy camp; *Bangdapgwiseon* (Lee Eon-ryang), in Bangdap; and the *Suncheongwiseon* (Park Yi-ryang), in Suncheon.

The inventor of Yi's geobukseon is commonly believed to be naval officer Na Dae-yong, who drew inspiration for its design from Goryeo dynasty warships and prototypes for a covered ship from the early Joseon era. The geobukseon was about the size of a panokseon, with a similar crew

This drawing of geobukseon was derived from drawings in the *Yi Chungmugong Chronicles*, a collection of the complete works of the admiral, published in 1795 under the direction of King Jeongjo. The drawing displays two variations of the geobukseon: the *Jwasuyeong* (Left Navy) geobukseon at the top and *Tongjeyeong* geobukseon below it. The chronicles state that the Tongjeyeong design is closer to the one used by Yi. Modern depictions of the geobukseon have the dragon head protruding upwards, with assertions that it spouted sulphuric smoke. This variation of the geobukseon was likely developed under King Jeongjo. According to the chronicles, the geobukseon had 24 rooms in the lower deck, of which two were used for storage, three as armouries and 19 for crew quarters. (Seokdang Museum of Dong-A University)

complement. In spite of its importance, we do not, and likely will never know, what Yi's geobukseon exactly looked like. Yi's nephew Yi Il gives the most detailed description:

> And he [Yi] created another warship, the size of which was like a panokseon, the top was covered with planks, a cross-shaped narrow passage was made on the planks for people to walk through, and the rest of the part was all filled with knives and awls so that there was no place to set foot in any direction, and in the front he created a dragon's head with gun holes, and in the back he created a turtle's tail with gun holes underneath it as well, and on each side there were six gun holes. In general, because its shape resembled a turtle, he named it 'gwiseon'.

The geobukseon has since entered military myth as a 16th-century wonder weapon, with claims that it was the world's first ironclad warship with an iron-plated roof covered in spikes. However, more likely than not, the geobukseon was not an ironclad vessel. Neither Yi nor any contemporary Joseon records reference any sort of armour plating on the roof. Samuel Hawley suggests the negative space of evidence, that amidst Yi's meticulous records of his fleet's use of precious metal, there is no mention of any quantity being used to plate the roof of the geobukseon. The geobukseon was possibly reinforced with armour in a few areas, but probably not the entire roof – the Japanese naval report on the battle of Angolpo mentions that 'among the large ships, three were turtle ships, and they were reinforced with iron at strong points'.

Another key point of controversy has been whether the geobukseon was two or three levels – whether it was a low-lying assault craft or essentially a covered panokseon. The strongest evidence in favour of the former is the presence of a covered spiked roof to prevent boarding, which would have been unnecessary as a three-level Joseon ship would have stood taller than most Japanese ships. Given the lack of information both sides had on each other's naval capabilities, it is plausible that Yi added the spikes as a precautionary measure rather than a reactionary one. Indeed, later drawings and accounts of the geobukseon seem to leave out the spikes, so it is possible that these were removed after initial encounters with the Japanese but the roof kept for its protection against indirect arquebus and arrow fire. Another argument against the two-level model is that it would have forced the gun and oar deck to be uncomfortably cramped since Joseon oars were manned standing – indeed contemporary reconstructions of the two-level model leave very little room between the massive oars and cannons interspersed between them.

The geobukseon had about 8–10 oars, coming out of the overhang of the second deck, as they were rowed standing. There were 14 guns on the upper deck (one in the dragon's mouth, one in the stern and six on each side), but the ship was designed to be able to fight on all sides simultaneously, so its artillery crew would have been about the same or slightly greater than that of a panokseon. The dragon's head fired a Hyeonja chongtong from its mouth, while the heavier guns were emplaced on the side. An open part ran through the middle of the wooden roof, enabling archers and crew to look out. Na Dae-yong noted that it was inconvenient to shoot arrows from the ship, yet the ship did have a complement of archers.

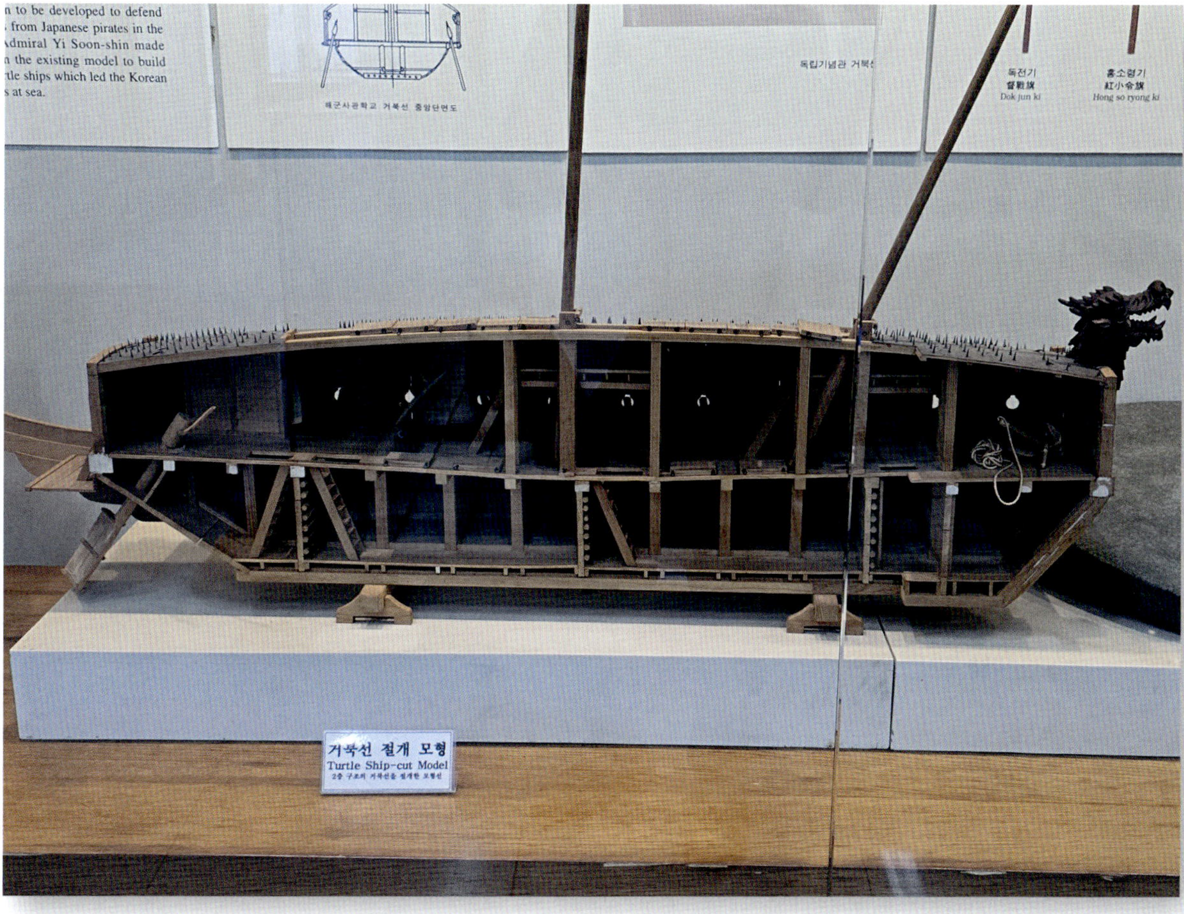

ABOVE
A cross-section of the two-level geobukseon, which is how the ship is seen in the public memory. One can see how even in this model there is little room for both cannons and oars. The ship has a built-in intermediary deck that allows access to the open section on the roof, to be used by archers. (Photograph by Kim Min-su, Okpo Battle Memorial Park)

LEFT
The *ho-go*, a large drum used by the Joseon military. These would have been mounted on command ships and used for signalling in battle or ceremonial purposes. Typically, the Joseon navy used a complex system of flags to relay orders and formation changes. The drum would have been used for coordination purposes or rallying troops. (Photograph by Kim Min-su, Okpo Battle Memorial Park)

The Joseon fleet employed a variety of naval formations for use in different situations, including long columns and general battle lines. The most prominent formation was the *hagik-jin*, the 'crane's wing formation'. The hagik-jin formed ships out into a massive arc to maximize their firepower and strike the enemy from the flanks. Its weakness was that the formation was relatively narrow, and as such, Yi employed his geobukseon to break up the Japanese formations before deploying the hagik-jin, and at times only used the formation for the initial attack before ordering his ships to close in. Communication between ships was done by a combination of drum signals, horns and flags.

Intelligence gathering was vital for Yi's operations. The Joseon navy had in its employ *hyeopseon*, small auxiliary boats used for non-combat purposes such as reconnaissance. These had crews of around five men each and could be equipped with signal rockets. Yi also sometimes dispatched small teams of officers to scout the Japanese bases, but the most valuable information came from Japanese deserters or rescued Korean prisoners, who could report on the detailed state of affairs inside the camps.

JAPANESE

Hideyoshi's navy had its origins in regional clan navies or Wako pirates who were absorbed into the forces of daimyos. The navy was formed according to the following decrees:

1. Two large ships should be prepared by each of the counties along the sea from Hitachi in the east through the Southern Sea to Shikoku and Kyushu, and from Sakata in Akita to Chugoku in the north.
2. Ten sailors from every 100 houses in each port are to be sent to work the large ships, and if there were any extra sailors, they are to come to Osaka.
3. For each 100,000 koku of land in the Tenryo [central territories under Hideyoshi's direct control] three large ships and five medium-sized ships should be built.

On paper, the naval contingent numbered some 9,200 soldiers, led by daimyos Kuki Yoshitaka (1,500), Todo Takatora (2,000), Wakizaka Yasuharu (1,500), Kato Yoshiaki (750), Kurushima Michiyuki and Michifusa (700), with the forces of Suga Tatsunaga, Kuwayama Shigekatsu and Horiuchi Ujiyoshi making up the remainder. These were far too few by themselves to have operated the hundreds of ships in Hideyoshi's armada, and the actual number of sailors was far greater than just the troops of the naval daimyos. Stephen Turnbull's analysis of Goto Sumiharu's 705-man contingent in the 1st Division reveals that 200 were boatmen, indicating that the transport crews that Yi faced often belonged to individual land contingents rather than the dedicated naval units. Perhaps most critically, Hideyoshi's navy had no overall commander, and the regional clan navies reported independently to Hideyoshi's headquarters at Nagoya. The martial prowess of the samurai leading the divisions is well known and needs no explanation here. War always brought opportunities for personal glory for the samurai to rise up the social ladder, but such was the senseless slaughter in Korea that some samurai, most notably Sayaga and 500 of his men, even deserted to join the Joseon army. The average Japanese ashigaru infantryman or sailor was conscripted and the war, too, provided him an opportunity for either glory or plunder. However, as the war entered an attritional phase, desertion became rife. We have an excellent profile of one such ashigaru, a 25-year old arquebusier named Magohichi from Shikoku. He was a slave who had been promised freedom if he joined the army due to his skill in archery. He was sent to Korea with 600 men as replacements to Chosokabe Motochika, whose contingent had been wracked with desertions. When he found only starvation and none of the riches he was promised, Magohichi and his friend Yasaburo deserted, but the latter was caught. Magohichi managed to escape to the coast, where he was captured by a trio of refugee women, Segum, Kumdae and Tokji, who trounced him when they came upon him while searching for oysters and turned him over to Na Dae-yong. After interrogation, Yi wanted to execute him on suspicion of being a spy, but he was instead handed over to the custody of the regular army command.

Hideyoshi relegated the naval arm of his invasion force to a distant secondary role to the ground troops. Indeed, the first order of business for the

With the promulgation of firearms in the 16th century, Japanese armour design underwent a shift from ornate webs of lacing and iron scales to more practical plate-based armour. This example falls under the *okegawa-do* class of armour (meaning tub, in reference to its similar construction method to a wooden bathtub rather than its shape). The armour plates in this samurai armour are held together by intricate *hishinui* stitching. (From the collection of the Jinju National Museum, accessible at https://www.emuseum.go.kr/)

This Japanese *haramaki* (breastplate only) armour blends several traditional armour styles together. The base is of *kusari* (chainmail), with the chest area woven by *kikko* hexagonal plates (iron or leather). The *kusazuri* (thigh guards), however, use the *karuta* style of square plates. (From the collection of the Jinju National Museum, accessible at https://www.emuseum.go.kr/)

A model of an *O-atakebune*, possibly *Nihon Maru*. Lightly armoured and highly decorated, such a ship would not have been designed for combat, rather for ceremonial purposes. It is entirely within the realm of possibility that both depictions of *Nihon Maru* – this unarmoured one and the one resembling a larger atakebune – are correct as the wooden walls could have been added or removed. Nonetheless, Hideyoshi's navy at the outset of the invasion was composed of a myriad of ships, most of which were not dedicated warships. (From the Ikunoshin Kadono Memorial Museum in Toba City, Japan)

navy was transportation, not combat. Hideyoshi did make an unsuccessful attempt in 1585 to hire two Portuguese galleons to aid his invasion, but he seems to have been not particularly concerned with the Joseon navy, especially once the Gyeongsang navies self-destructed and a foothold had been established in Busan. Upon landfall, many of the naval commanders were immediately given inland assignments, and the minor daimyos who had organized the transports now found themselves free to act as Wako pirates once more.

Japanese ships were made of cedar and much more streamlined than Korean ships, as their hulls were in a 'v shape' that let them cut through water without resistance while moving forwards. The downside was that the ships were less manoeuvrable when moving at speed. Additionally, the ships of the invasion force were likely not of great quality. Between Hideyoshi's official announcement of his plan to invade Korea on 9d 3m 1591, to the invasion launch date about a year later, Japan needed to produce over 1,000 ships. Many daimyos undoubtedly patched together existing ships in disrepair to meet their quotas rather than build new ones. Cedar, while soft and easy to work with, is less durable than other woods, and the iron nails used in the construction of Japanese ships tended to rust, whereas Joseon ships used wooden pegs.

While there were three classes of Japanese warship designs, construction was not standardized across the entire fleet, so individual ships varied greatly in measurement. Small fast boats used for reconnaissance, communication and other minor tasks were known as *kobaya* – these had a crew of 30 or less. The *sekibune* was a medium-sized warship, one or two storeys tall with a crew of around 50–60. At times bamboo shields

A model of a Kuki clan O-atakebune of the kind he used at the second battle of Kizugawaguchi. Emblazoned on the sail is the Hidari Mitsudomoe, the triple black circles used by Kuki as his family crest. This symbol would have adorned other banners and flags on his ships. (From the Ikunoshin Kadono Memorial Museum in Toba City, Japan)

were attached to the sides to provide additional protection for the crews. The next class of Japanese warship was the atakebune. These were usually three-level ships averaging 28m long, and had a pavilion-like structure on their decks where the commander resided or a deck house that was used to house arquebusiers. Its crew complement was around 140, of which 60 were infantry. The largest of the Japanese warships were O-atakebune, essentially massive atakebune, and one of these, *Nihon Maru*, would participate in the Imjin War.

It was certainly not the case that Japanese naval forces in the late 16th century were devoid of any vessels with ship-to-ship combat capability. Under orders from Hideyoshi, the Kuki clan constructed six sturdy O-atakebune ships that were heavily armed with artillery.

These O-atakebune routed the 600-ship-strong Mori clan navy at the 1578 battle of Kizugawaguchi. However, this was the exception rather than the norm, and naval battles were quite rare during the Sengoku era. Japanese naval doctrine was informed through the role of warships in Sengoku-era warfare. The Japanese clans typically used their navies along the coast in combined-arms operations with ground forces, acting as transports or blockading castles in sieges. When ships did come into contact with each other, combat was essentially a translation of land tactics, with crews using volley fire and boarding tactics – victory was achieved not by sinking the enemy ship but by eliminating its crew.

Firearms had promulgated heavily in Japan with the introduction of the *teppo* (arquebus) by Portuguese merchants in 1543, quickly becoming a staple ingredient of Japanese infantry tactics. Cannon, however, had yet to be widely adopted for naval use. It was only in response to his defeats in 1592 that Hideyoshi would order the construction of larger and sturdier ships capable of mounting cannon. The Japanese did use the *Ozutsu teppo*, a heavier arquebus operated by a two- or three-man crew, depending on the size. Larger versions were mounted on wheels and functioned essentially as light cannon. One Korean officer noted, 'It has the power of a cannon, and its accuracy is as good as an arquebus, making it truly unstoppable.' Joseon officials were thoroughly impressed by the penetration power and powder efficiency of the Ozutsu teppo they captured, and requested they be reproduced.

Headhunting was a common measure of military performance among Ming China, Japan and Joseon Korea. While Yi meticulously notes this practice and the number of heads that subordinates took, it is clear that he was well aware of the tactical detriment this practice could have by distracting soldiers from combat. He made sure to make note of subordinates who had taken no heads because they were too busy fighting, and often reserved trophy collection for after the battle. Yi told his men:

> If you compete with one another in cutting off the heads of the dead enemy to gain merit or reward, you are more likely to increase casualties on our side. I promise to recommend those who fight best by killing the enemy by shooting as expert marksmen, even if they cut off no heads of the enemy dead. You are expected to obey my command.

The arquebus first entered Japan in 1543 when Lord Tanegashima Toitaka purchased two from Portuguese merchants and set about reproducing them. While artillery, rockets and hand cannons had long been popular in East Asian militaries, the gunpowder frenzy failed to take hold in Japan until the 16th century. In contrast to European arquebuses, Japanese arquebuses had a shorter stock that was placed against the cheek rather than the shoulder. Additionally, Japanese, and later Korean, arquebuses were of the snap matchlock variety, where the trigger was connected to a spring that held back the serpentine, whereby the gun fired instantaneously to the trigger pull. In contrast, European armies favoured use of the gradual-ignition matchlock, whereby the serpentine was directly connected to the trigger and came down as the trigger was pulled. This particular arquebus was likely used only for ceremonial purposes. (From the collection of the National Museum of Korea, accessible at https://www.emuseum.go.kr/)

THE CAMPAIGNS

THE FIRST CAMPAIGN: OKPO

News of the armageddon that befell Joseon reached Yi at dusk on 15d 4m, in the form of a report from Won Gyun that 90 Japanese ships were before Busan. Moments later, he received another letter from Park Hong that there were 350 ships. Yi sprang into action, dispatching a flurry of messages to his subordinates and passing word to the Jeolla Right Navy. The next day, at 2200hrs, he learned from another letter by Won Gyun that Busan had fallen. His immediate reaction was one of heartbreak and anger at the defeat. Further reports on the 17th day confirmed that the Japanese were landing more troops, meaning that this was no simple pirate raid. Such reports continued to flow in for the next several days, and Yi busied himself with fortifying the naval base and surrounding garrisons, and recruiting more soldiers – some 700 volunteers came on the 19th. On the 20th, Yi received a letter from Yeongnam magistrate Kim Su with information that the Japanese were advancing inland. Yi was distressed at Kim's words that 'many enemies are rushing in, and we cannot stop them'. Kim also wrote that he had ordered Won Gyun to take his fleet out to sea, and asked Yi to ready his fleet to be on standby. However, without royal orders, Yi could not leave Jeolla Province.

On the 23rd, Yi finally received royal orders to join with Won Gyun as soon as possible. Given the rapidly changing situation, the Joseon court also granted Yi and other provincial commanders the freedom to act on their own initiative. However, Yi realized that a crisis of this magnitude could not be left to individual contingents to rush in and be defeated in detail, and that a centralized command needed to be maintained. Yi requested 'the continued import of royal instructions'. He 'also requested Gyeongsang Border Defence General Yi Il, Governor Kim Su, and Naval Station Commander Won Gyun to immediately send charts showing the waterways in their province, in addition to other data including expected rendezvous of naval units of the two provinces, the numbers of the enemy vessels and the locations of their present anchorages, plus strategic recommendations'.

In the meantime, Yi gave the order for his captains to assemble at Yeosu, estimating that he could have a fighting force ready by the 29th. He was determined to 'make surprise attacks on them [the Japanese], displaying our martial spirit and firepower in order to strike terror deep into their hearts'. Yi only called for the squadrons in his land administrative counties,

A drawing of Song Hui-rip, at the Chungmusa shrine in Suncheon. Song served under Yi throughout the war until the final battle at Noryang. He eventually rose to the position of Jeolla Left Navy Jeoldosa. (From the Suncheon Tourism Association)

noting that those units were well organized whereas the flotillas at smaller bases were 'scattered and weak'. Yi also asked Yi Eok-gi to join him by 30d 4m. In the meantime, Won clashed with the advancing Japanese navy, reportedly sinking ten ships. However, on the 29th, Yi received an alarming message from Won, saying that the Japanese were far too strong and that he had lost his naval base. As a result, Won hoped to combine forces with Yi at Dangpo. Some of Yi's subordinates opposed leaving Jeolla undefended, others surely thought that to sail to Gyeongsang against an enemy that had defeated the Gyeongsang navies was suicide. Yi Eok-gi had yet to arrive, and the geobukseon were not yet ready for combat. What could they do with just 24 ships against 500? However, others favoured aggressive action. Song Hui-rip vehemently argued, 'Is Gyeongsang not also our land? The best way to defend Jeolla is to defeat the enemy before they attack.' On 3d 5m, Jeong Un requested to meet with Yi privately and stated that if they did not sail now, they may not have such an opportunity again. Yi decided that he would sail to Won Gyun's aid, regardless of what lay ahead, and he and his captains gathered to swear that they would fight to the death.

In the fifth lunar month of 1592, Joseon Korea was in chaos. The Japanese army was pushing northwards relentlessly, and the main royal army had been annihilated to a man at the disastrous battle of Chungju (Tangeumdae). Panic had gripped the Joseon armed forces. Garrison posts were abandoned without a fight, their soldiers scattering into the mountains. When the order was given to prepare to set sail, even veteran soldiers attempted to desert from Yi's naval base, and Yi had two of them executed and their heads displayed in an attempt to deter further desertions. For the civilian population, the consequences were disastrous. Most of the ships that Yi encountered on his initial sorties were the transports of Hideyoshi's armada, whose crews, after

The first campaign, 4d–9d 5m

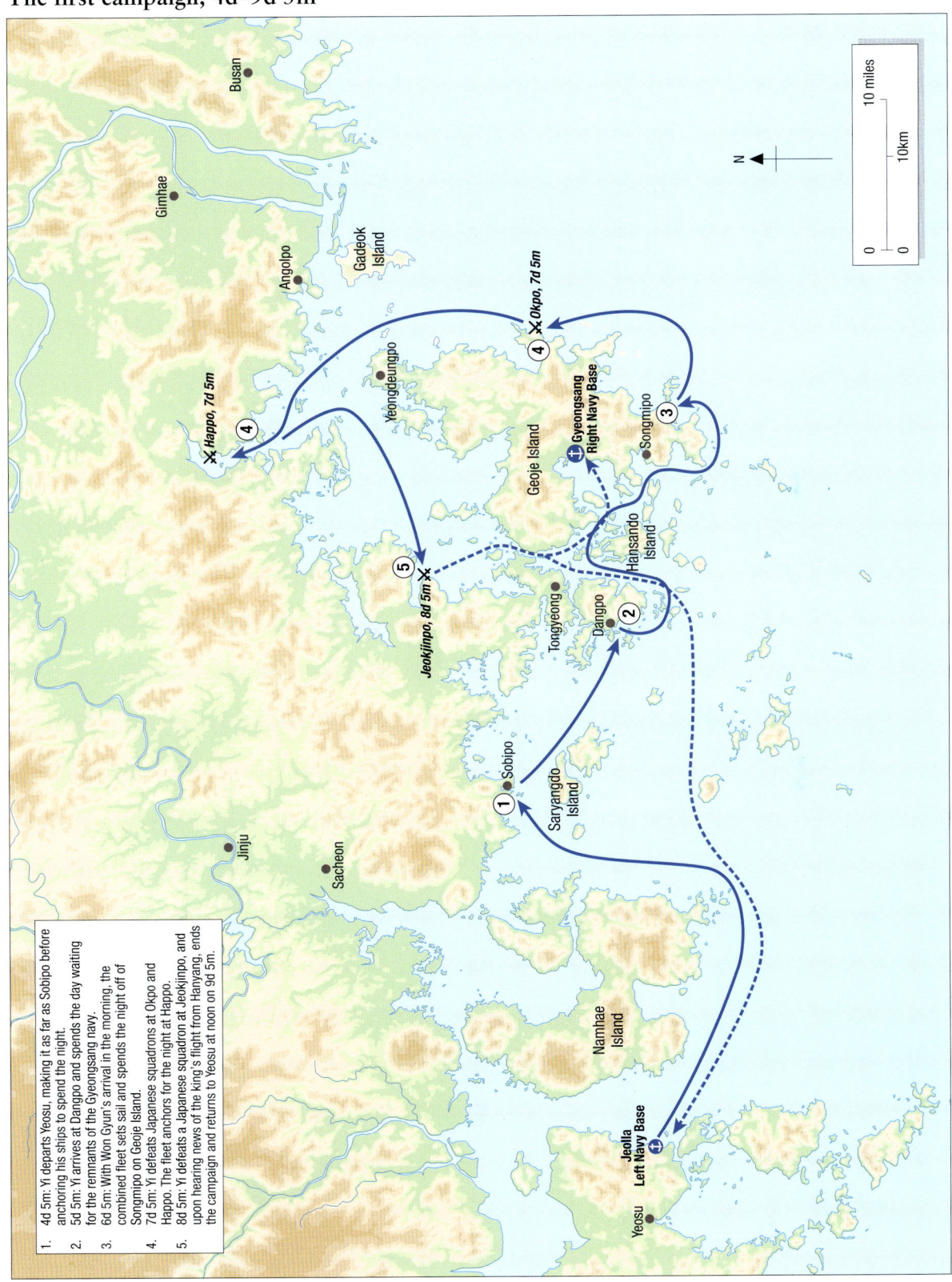

1. 4d 5m: Yi departs Yeosu, making it as far as Sobipo before anchoring his ships to spend the night.
2. 5d 5m: Yi arrives at Dangpo and spends the day waiting for the remnants of the Gyeongsang navy.
3. 6d 5m: With Won Gyun's arrival in the morning, the combined fleet sets sail and spends the night off of Songmipo on Geoje Island.
4. 7d 5m: Yi defeats Japanese squadrons at Okpo and Happo. The fleet anchors for the night at Happo.
5. 8d 5m: Yi defeats a Japanese squadron at Jeokjinpo, and upon hearing news of the king's flight from Hanyang, ends the campaign and returns to Yeosu at noon on 9d 5m.

landing their troops in Busan, pillaged, raped and slaughtered their way westward in coastal raids. Yi writes:

> The outrages of the enemy have reached the height of cruelty: killing, kidnapping, and plundering, making countless homeless orphans. During my recent inspection trip throughout the coastal areas, I found everywhere large groups of wandering refugees, young and old, who at the sight of our ships sobbed and cried for help, and furnished information on the movements of the enemy. They were so tragically pitiful that I felt like carrying them all on our ships, but there were too many of them and it would be difficult for the fighting vessels to navigate with full loads of refugees on board.

Yi and his troops made their best efforts to assist these refugees – many would eventually settle around the security of the Yeosu base – and the assistance went both ways as the refugees and freed prisoners would become Yi's primary source of intelligence on the movements of Japanese ships.

Yi's fleet departed Yeosu on the morning of 4d 5m, without Yi Eok-gi. Yi had planned to resupply, rearm and collect reinforcements from Namhae, but he found the town abandoned by its garrison and devoid of supplies. Undeterred, the fleet sailed on, anchoring and spending the night near modern-day Goseong. The sailors slept on the decks at battle stations. The next day, the fleet sailed to Dangpo, where, finding no one, Yi sent a message to Won Gyun. The remnants of the Gyeongsang Right Navy arrived in dribs and drabs, with Won Gyun himself arriving the morning of the 6th with a single panokseon. In all, Won Gyun had with him just three panokseon and a smattering of auxiliary craft. As it turned out, Won Gyun had scuttled most of his fleet. Unable to defeat the Japanese navy, Won Gyun, or one of his subordinates, had scattered the crews and sunk the 70 ships in the Gyeongsang Right Navy rather than let them fall into the hands of the Japanese. Won, however, had much more time to prepare his men than Park Hong did. Won's scuttling of his fleet would define his relationship with Yi for the coming campaigns, as he was relegated to a secondary role in spite of his marginal seniority by age. The realization that they were alone in this fight must have been a hard blow to the morale of Yi's men.

Screening Yi's panokseon was a cloud of hyeopseon that served as his ears and eyes, coordinated by Sado and Yeodo squadron commanders Kim Wan and Kim In-young. Soon enough, one of these boats fired a signal rocket from Okpo, on Geoje Island. More intel flooded in of a Japanese squadron of 50 ships flying red banners that lay at anchor in Okpo bay. Reiterating to his captains to follow his orders, and to act with sangfroid and caution, Yi set sail for Okpo on the 7th. It is uncertain who the Japanese commander at Okpo was. Japanese naval records list Todo Takatora as the commander, but the Todo family history contradicts this, as it records that Todo entered Korea for the first time in the seventh month carrying orders from Hideyoshi dictating a change in naval strategy. Likely, we will never know who commanded the squadron at Okpo. In any case, the Japanese crews had disembarked to pillage, such that smoke from burning houses marked their position. The Japanese were utterly oblivious and unprepared when Yi's fleet sailed to the mouth of the harbour. They had thought the Joseon navy to be all but destroyed, having encountered no opposition

A painting of the battle of Okpo. The oars of the panokseon are depicted coming out from the side of the hull, while traditional Korean oars would have emerged from an overhang and been rowed standing. (From the Korean Naval Academy Museum)

to their initial landing and subsequent raids along the coast. Seeing the unfurled sails emerging in the distance, the Japanese dashed back to their ships, loaded their arquebuses and prepared to charge their unexpected opponents. However, they never got the opportunity to do so. Yi halted his ships in a battle line some distance from the Japanese ships, turning 90 degrees, in position to broadside.

Yi gave the order to fire, and his panokseon launched a fusillade of shot hurtling towards the Japanese ships. Japanese morale collapsed at the impact of the cannonade as splinters flew and ships were reduced to bloody wrecks. Yi's gunners carefully aimed their pieces to hit their opponents just at the waterline. Some six Japanese ships attempted to charge, but they were quickly reduced to shattered wrecks. Yoon Baek-nyeon, the 14-year old daughter of a Gyeongsang Left Navy sailor, held captive on board a Japanese ship, recounted after her rescue:

> cannon balls and long arrows poured down like hail on the Japanese vessels from our ships. Those who were struck by the missiles fell dead, bathed in blood, while others rolled on deck with wild shrieks or jumped into the water to climb up the hills. At that time I remained motionless with fear at the bottom of the boat for long hours so I did not know what happened in the outside world.

Yi decided to seal his victory and ordered his hyeopseon forward. These smaller ships dashed into the smoke-filled bay, towards what remained of the Japanese squadron, firing fire-arrows to finish off the wrecked ships in the shallows and picking off sailors struggling in the water. The Japanese

This display at the Korean National Museum of Science and Technology in Daejeon depicts a variety of Joseon weapons as they would have been seen in action. A mannequin of a Joseon soldier holds a complete Seungja chongtong; behind him a hwacha fires a volley of shingijeon arrows. (Photograph by Yuhan Kim, from the Korea National Science Museum)

force was in rout, with many fleeing to the shore, while others hugged the coastline with their ships to manoeuvre past Yi's battle line. The Japanese lost 26 ships and several hundred men. The Jeolla Left Navy sunk 13 atakebune, six sekibune and two small ships, while the Gyeongsang Right Navy sunk five atakebune. Yi, for his part, suffered just one marine injured – for the Joseon navy, this battle had played out like a drill with live ammunition. Okpo was the first major Joseon victory in the Imjin War, and did much to restore the broken morale of Yi's men. Yi even sought to send his marines inland to finish off the Japanese stragglers, but concerns that the Japanese could counterattack convinced him to sail to Yeongdeungpo on Geoje Island to rest and refit. Yi sent Yoon and a rescued orphaned toddler to Suncheon with a request to be looked after.

They were hardly given a moment's rest when another signal rocket was spotted in the distance. Sailing towards Happo, the Joseon fleet caught five atakebune in the harbour. Unable to respond to the Korean barrage, the Japanese sailors abandoned their ships and fled inland. Yi burned the ships and sailed his fleet to Nampo. The next day, 8d 5m, saw a repeat of the previous engagements when Yi's fleet caught a squadron of 13 Japanese ships of mostly atakebune anchored at Jeokjinpo. Here, too, the crews were busy pillaging nearby villages and thus put up little resistance when Yi's fleet approached. Eleven ships were sunk at Jeokjinpo, with no Korean losses.

This photograph, taken from Dongbu-myeon on Geoje Island, looks east with Hansando Island in the distance. While the battlefield is not visible in this photograph, it captures the nature of the terrain where Yi campaigned. (Photograph by Kim Young-soo, Korea Tourism Organization)

For officers such as Park Yeong-nam and Kim Bong-su, the victory was even more significant as their homes were in Jeokjinpo.

Angered by the plight of a Korean refugee who left the safety of the naval force to search for his missing wife and children, Yi's captains wanted to follow up on their victories by attacking known Japanese concentrations at Gadeok Island and Busan. However, Yi did not want to fight in shallow water advantageous to the enemy and, moreover, he still needed to reunite with the Jeolla Right Navy. As Yi, Won Gyun and their officers discussed what to do next, their fleet received well-deserved rest, replenishing and rearming from the mass of supplies taken from the Japanese ships. It was then that Yi received word that the Joseon capital of Hanyang had fallen, and that King Seonjo had fled northward. Shocked and distressed, the officers decided to return to base to better address the shifting strategic situation on land. Yi writes, 'They were so shocked and indignant that they held each other all day long, feeling as if their insides were being torn apart, and they cried and shed tears all at once.' To give his government a glimmer of good news, Yi dispatched news of his victories, along with heads taken as trophies, and captured weapons and armour. However, a rift began to form between Won and Yi. Won wanted to submit a joint battle report, and Yi refused, understandably because Won Gyun had hardly contributed to his victories. Additionally, Yi condemned Won Gyun's lack of control over his troops in his report because of a friendly fire incident where Won's men had fired arrows at a Japanese ship being boarded by Yi's men, wounding two marines. From then on, the two men would submit their own battle reports to the court.

THE SECOND CAMPAIGN: SACHEON, DANGPO AND DANGHANGPO

Yi kept his fleet in harbour for two weeks, training, repairing and receiving reports of the national situation with trepidation. However, with increasing reports of Japanese raids, Yi could no longer wait for official orders to act. He sent a message to Yi Eok-gi telling him to hurry so that

The second campaign, 29d 5m–9d 6m

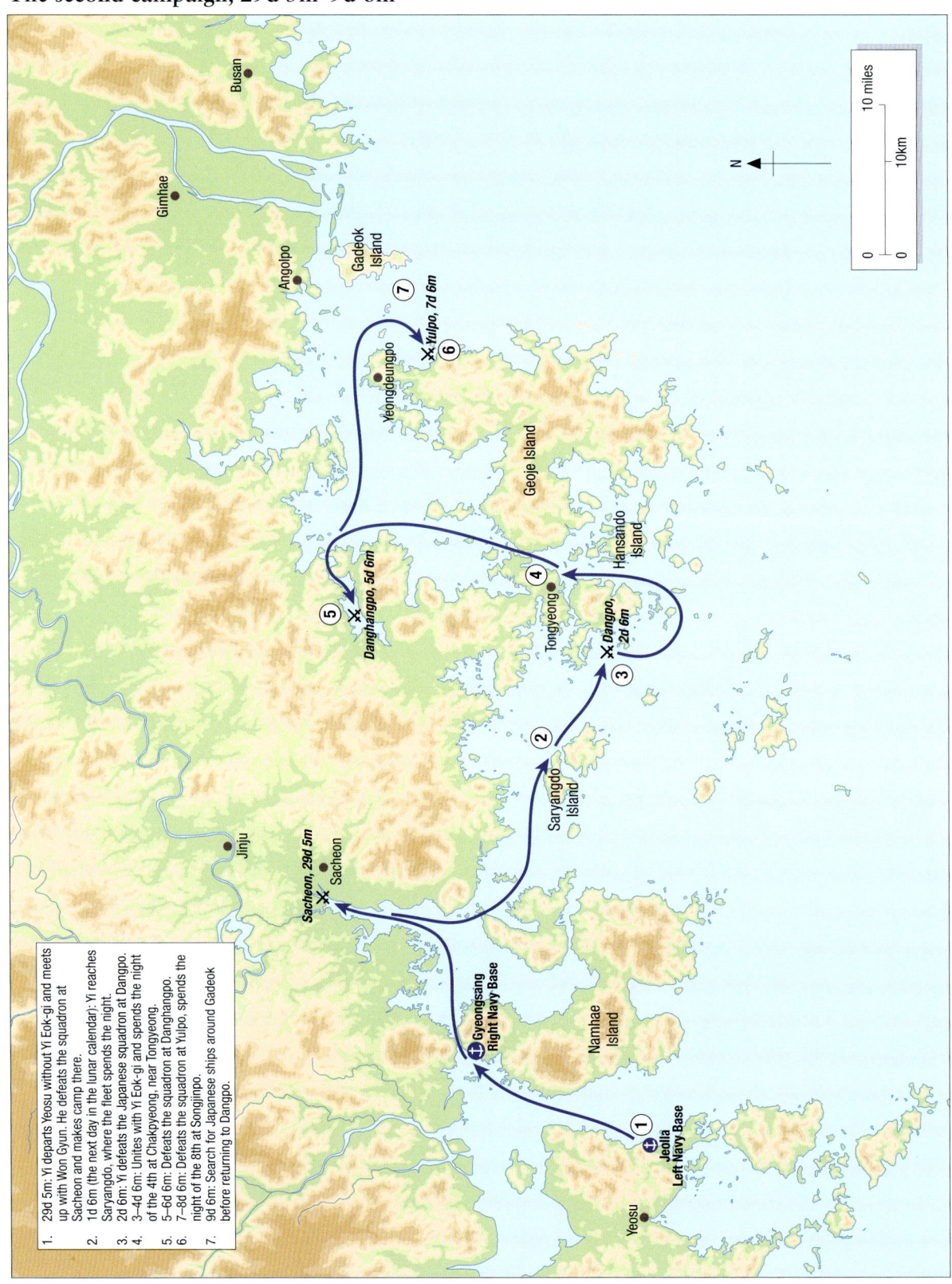

they could join forces and launch another sortie, only to be informed on the 26th that Yi Eok-gi would only be able to arrive at Yeosu by 3d 6m. The opportunity for battle came much sooner when Won Gyun reported on the 27d 5m that he had moved his base to Noryang after encountering Japanese ships at Sacheon. Concerned that the Japanese would effect a larger concentration by the following month, Yi pushed forward his planned sortie and set sail on the 29th, without Yi Eok-gi. This time, Yi brought with him his completed geobukseon, though he left behind one (most likely the *Suncheongwiseon*) along with several panokseon under the 80-year-old Jeong Geol, his chief of staff, to guard Yeosu in his absence.

Yi met with Won Gyun at Noryang that same day, with their combined force moving to intercept the squadron at Sacheon. In all, Yi had 21–23 panokseon and two geobukseon, while Won Gyun had three panokseon. The geobukseon were put into a provisional squadron under Flying Squadron Chief Lee Gi-nam, the captain of the *Yeonggwiseon*. Yi's second-in-command was Suncheon magistrate Kwon Jun, the centre squadron was led by Gwangyang County magistrate Eo Yeong-dam, the left by Shin Ho, the right by Kim Deuk-gwang and the rear by Hongyang County magistrate Bae Hong-rip. The Joseon vanguard pursued and sank a scout ship before Sacheon, though its crew escaped onto land. At Sacheon, Yi found a dozen atakebune and some smaller boats, while some 400 Japanese had disembarked to build fortifications and encampments on the ridges beyond the coast. The terrain proved quite disadvantageous – the Japanese were far enough inland that they were out of range of the Joseon fleet, while the receding tide made it difficult to pull in close to the Japanese ships and burn them. Yi decided to try a feigned retreat, and reiterated to his captains to stick with the plan. The Joseon fleet pulled back about half a kilometre, and the Japanese took the bait – 200 Japanese rushed down from their mountaintop positions to man the ships, while the other half took up positions closer to the coast and began firing at Yi's ships. At a signal, the Joseon ships turned around to spring the trap. With the evening tide at their backs and adding speed to their charge, the pair of geobukseon dived into the pursuing Japanese and sprayed cannon fire everywhere. The geobukseon came under small-arms fire from naval troops and the coastal positions, but the crew were well protected under its wooden armour (except for Na Dae-yong, who was slightly wounded, perhaps while excitedly trying to get a better view of his invention in action). Seeing Korean collaborators in the midst of the Japanese ranks, the angered Yi sailed his flagship at full speed straight into the disarrayed Japanese formation, spraying flechettes and cannonballs everywhere. His squadron commanders soon followed, sinking the rest of the Japanese ships. The surviving Japanese crews fled inland, their retreat covered by nightfall. During the fighting, Yi was shot in the left shoulder, but it fortunately proved to be a minor wound. Only four other Koreans were wounded in the action (including Na Dae-yong).

As usual, Yi left intact two small boats in the hope that the Japanese would take them and try to escape into open water, where he could catch them. The next day, dated 1d 6m on the lunar calendar, Won Gyun went back to Sacheon to collect heads from the corpses and to try and hunt down the survivors. But finding that they had fled inland, Won could do little but burn the two boats. With barely enough ships, crew and weapons to amount

Admiral Yi's wounding at the battle of Sacheon, as portrayed in a painting displayed at the Jeseungdang. Yi is said to have ignored the wound until the battle was over, after which a subordinate performed a battlefield surgery by extracting the bullet with a sword point. (Courtesy of the Jeseungdang)

to an effective fighting force, the Gyeongsang Right Navy was relegated to clean-up operations.

At 0800hrs on 2d 6m, Yi received information of a Japanese force at Dangpo, and set sail without hesitation, arriving there at 1000hrs. At Dangpo, there were 21 ships flying yellow banners anchored at the bay, commanded by Tokui Michiyugi (also known as Kurushima Michiyuki), the older brother of naval daimyo Kurushima Michifusa. Nine of them were atakebune, comparable to the panokseon, while the others were sekibune

Deep-seated in Korean tradition and history, archery remains a popular sport in Korea. The traditional Korean composite bow was made from horn and wood, from which it drew its tension. Here the bow is in its unstrung form, and the inward curved ends would be drawn back and strung. (From the collection of the National Museum of Korea, accessible at https://www.emuseum.go.kr/)

or smaller. Some 300 Japanese were on land. Half had broken into Dangpo Castle and were pillaging it, while the other half remained outside. The Joseon forces engaged immediately, with the geobukseon leading the attack. Tokui was killed, and Japanese morale collapsed. What was left of Tokui's command scattered inland, too shocked by their defeat to loot in their overland retreat. With superior firepower, Yi's fleet suffered no losses at Dangpo, while every Japanese ship was sunk.

Just as Yi prepared to dispatch parties in pursuit of the surviving Japanese, news arrived that another Japanese squadron of 20 atakebune from Geoje Island was anchored nearby. Yi raced to the scene, sticking to open water in the hopes of luring that squadron out to sea. However, by this point, word had got around of Yi's unstoppable fleet, and the Japanese squadron scattered. The heavier panokseon were unable to keep up, and with darkness settling, Yi called off the pursuit. Yi spent the next day, 3d 6m, searching the nearby inlets in vain.

The following day, a soldier named Kang Dak emerged from hiding in the mountains after seeing Yi's ships pass by and reported:

> After the battle at Dangpo, the surviving Japanese cut off the heads of their dead in large numbers and cremated them in one place, before they departed for the mainland. While escaping, they met our men, but far from killing us, they passed us without noticing, weeping bitterly. As for the Japanese vessels which you have been hunting as far as the outer sea of Dangpo, they sailed toward Geoje today.

This critical lead was followed up with more good news – sails on the horizon heralded the belated arrival of Yi Eok-gi's Jeolla Right Navy. For Yi's men, who had been fighting essentially isolated from the rest of the Joseon armed forces, this was an immense boost to their morale. The exhausted officers and sailors whooped and danced with joy at the arrival of reinforcements – 25 panokseon in all. For the rest of the day, Yi, Yi Eok-gi and Won caught up and strategized. There was little question as to who would command the combined fleet. Yi was 16 years senior to Yi Eok-gi, and though Won Gyun was 53, five years senior to Yi, he was in no position to claim any authority after scuttling his fleet.

On 5d 6m, residents of Geoje Island, including pre-war Japanese immigrants, rowed out to inform Yi that the squadron he had been hunting since 2d 6m was at Danghangpo. On the way, Yi established communications with a 1,000-strong cavalry force under Yu Sung-in, the magistrate of Haman. He, too, had been shadowing the Japanese squadron all the way to Danghangpo. Yi gained a little information from Yu on the terrain at Danghangpo, but lacking further key details, dispatched three ships to scout the terrain and, if possible, bait the Japanese out. The vanguard instead launched signal arrows for the rest of the fleet to follow, so, leaving four ships to guard the entrance, Yi sailed into Danghangpo bay, while the Jeolla Right Navy hid in ambush positions in a cove along the Danghangpo inlet. The mouth of Danghangpo bay was some three miles wide, and narrowed into a winding channel six miles long, making it a good hiding spot. But Danghangpo was not narrow or shallow enough to prevent the panokseon from fighting effectively – the Japanese were trapped, raising the question of why they had chosen such a poor location for battle. Legend has it that the

BATTLE OF DANGPO, 2D 6M 1592 (PP. 48–49)

Based on the wording in Yi's report, it was the *Yeonggwiseon* that spearheaded Yi's attack on Tokui Michiyugi's squadron. Yi describes the Japanese squadron and Tokui's atakebune flagship in his battle report:

> The Japanese squadron consisted of nine large vessels of equal size to our ships and 12 medium and small vessels, all pulled alongside the quay. On the deck of a large vessel was a tall pavilion of about three lengths, soaring high into the sky, surrounded by a red brocade curtain, embroidered with a large Chinese character 黃 [yellow] on all sides **[1]**. Inside the pavilion was a Japanese commander with a red parasol planted in front. He showed no fear, like a man resigned to death **[2]**.

A Korean woman named Ok-tae who had been captured and forced to be Tokui's concubine described Tokui to Yi:

> The Japanese commander was a tall strong man, aged about 30. By day he wore a yellow brocade robe and gold crown and sat upon his dais in the pavilion of his boat, and at night he retired to sleep in a luxurious bed spread with beautiful bed-clothes. Many Japanese from each boat came to see him morning and evening, bending their heads to await orders. He killed those who were disobedient without mercy.

Yi describes the geobukseon attack as follows: 'First, the geobukseon [*Yeonggwiseon*] dashed close to this pavilion vessel and fired the Hyeonja cannon from the dragon-mouth upward at the tower, **(3)** then shot Cheonja and Jija cannons, and broke the enemy ship. Next it struck many Japanese vessels floating behind with its shot and arrows.' Ok-tae recounted, 'On the day of the battle, arrows and bullets rained on the pavilion vessel where he sat. First he was hit on the brow but was unshaken, but when an arrow pierced his chest he fell down with a loud cry.' It was Kwon Jun (Yi's second-in-command at the time), driving his panokseon into the Japanese line, who delivered the fatal arrow. Joseon marines boarded Tokui's ship and retrieved his head as well as a golden fan inscribed with the name Kamei Korenori and Hideyoshi written as the giver. It was this that led Yi to mistakenly believe that he had killed Kamei, one of Hideyoshi's senior naval commanders.

The design of the geobukseon shown in the picture is based on the three-storey model. The geobukseon would likely have relied purely on its oars in battle and its sails would have been folded up to allow better visibility from the open area on the roof and to prevent them from catching fire. The spiked roof was covered with straws to conceal them from the enemy. The geobukseon was often thought to have been used to ram enemy ships, based on the wording in Yi's battle reports, but a contextual analysis of his language indicates that he more likely referred to intense close-range attacks than an actual ramming.

The battle of Danghangpo, 5d 6m

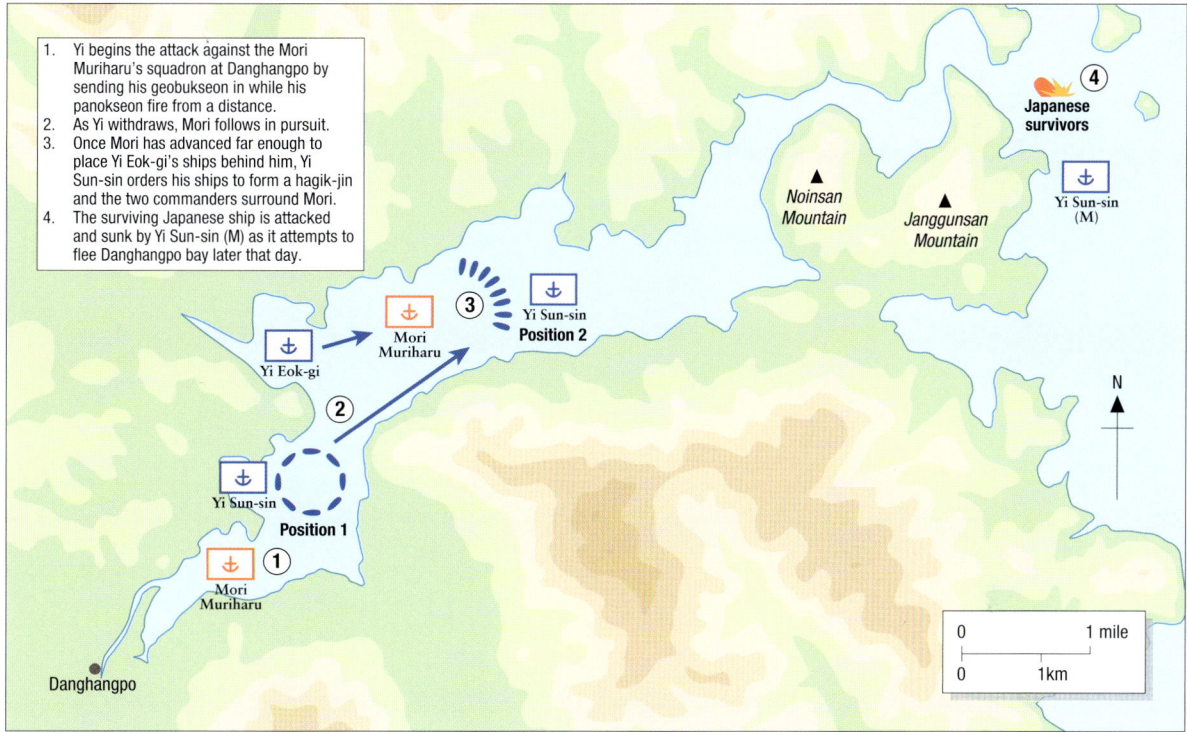

Japanese had been misled into Danghangpo. A year prior to the Imjin War, Japanese spies disguised as monks stayed at a *gisaeng* (courtesan) house. One of the gisaeng, Lee Yeol, deduced the true identity of her guests and with rumours abounding of an incoming Japanese invasion, Lee looked through their luggage and found a map. She sabotaged it by drawing a sea route to make it such that the Japanese believed the inlet was actually a strait that would lead them to open water on the other side. The Danghangpo squadron was operating on this assumption but instead found itself trapped.

The Japanese squadron at Danghangpo was part of the Awa navy and numbered nine atakebune, four sekibune and 13 small ships (kobaya or smaller sekibune) led by Mori Muriharu. The ships were painted black, flew black banners and had black sails, and according to Yi's official report, 'the largest was fitted out with a three-storied pavilion of wooden boards erected at the bow. This pavilion was painted in red, blue and white, like a Buddhist temple, with a green awning in front and a black-dyed brocade curtain drawn underneath. Behind the curtain embroidered with flower-crests a large number of Japanese stood ready.'

Four atakebune sailed forwards, displaying black banners with Buddhist chants inscribed on them, and their crews opened fire. Yi formed his ships up into a circle formation, spearheaded by Lee Gi-nam's *Yeonggwiseon*. The panokseon sailed in a circle, firing as they went, while the *Yeonggwiseon* closed in and punched gashes into the atakebune. Satisfied with having shattered the Japanese vanguard, Yi then broke off his naval carousel and ordered a feigned retreat to lure Mori's squadron to Yi Eok-gi's concealed ships. Seeking either to close with and board Yi Sun-sin's ships, or escape

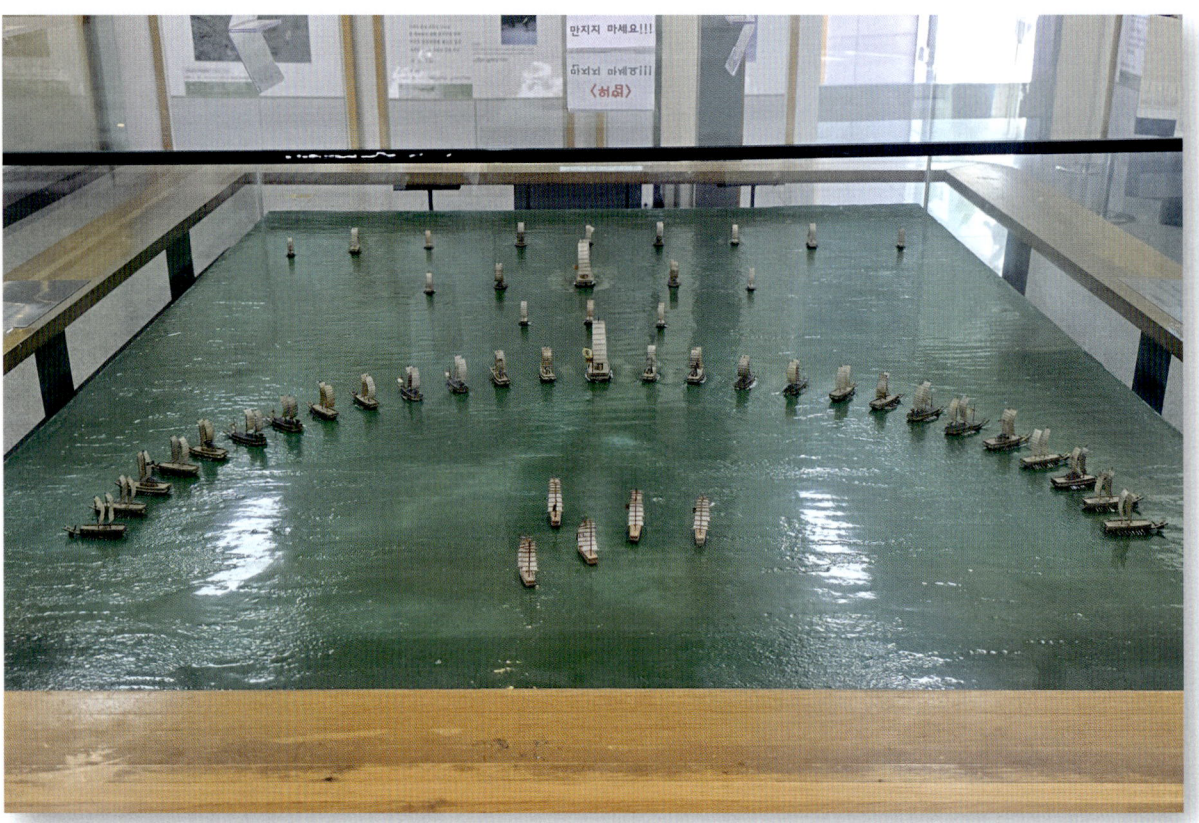

A diorama of the hagik-jin formation. Yi trained his men to use the formation in various iterations, either in fleet-wide manoeuvres or as squadrons forming smaller hagik-jin. (Photograph by Kim Min-su, Okpo Battle Memorial Park)

Danghangpo, Mori's squadron sped with their black sails unfurled, without noticing that they were putting Yi Eok-gi's hidden fleet right behind them. At a signal, Yi Sun-sin's ships reversed oars and halted to form a hagik-jin, and Yi Eok-gi's ships sailed out of the cove to form their own hagik-jin, surrounding Mori. Pummelled from all sides, the Japanese squadron was blasted out of the water. The geobukseon also sailed in, firing at the Japanese flagship, while marines shot flaming arrows at the magnificent sails and curtains to set the ships alight. Mori Muriharu was killed by an arrow, but his cousin, Mori Murashige, and Murashige's uncle, Shin Masashige, stepped up to command the faltering squadron, even recovering Mori's body. Seeing many armed Japanese sailors swim to shore, Yi ordered that one ship be left intact. Once again, the coming darkness prevented pursuit.

Yi waited for the Japanese to use the ship he had spared to escape, and sure enough they did. It was immediately trounced by Yi Sun-sin's (M) Bangdap squadron as it exited Danghangpo bay, smashed into a wreck by the cacophony of projectiles hurled at it. Amidst the sinking boat, one young samurai, clad in resplendent armour, is reported to have made a defiant last stand, surrounded by eight other soldiers, while the rest of the crew jumped overboard. This unnamed samurai could have been any of the Awa naval officers killed that day – Kashihara Ushinosuke, Komori Rokudayu, Awata Hanshichi or Watanabe Shikibu. The samurai fell after taking ten arrows, with Yi Sun-sin (M) delivering the *coup de grâce*, and his companions followed in quick succession. Yi's own losses in the battle were minor. Won Gyun's ships rowed to the scene of carnage and fished the bodies out of the water, collecting some 50 heads.

On 7d 6m, a Joseon scout ship reported finding a Japanese squadron at Yeongdeungpo on Geoje Island. Yi set out in pursuit, and the seven Japanese ships fled towards Gadeok Island as soon as they saw the Joseon ships emerging in the distance. They threw cargo overboard to gain speed, but because the easterly wind was too strong, they turned south. Yi's crew rowed madly and began to gain on the Japanese ships. Unable to escape, the Japanese beached their ships at Yulpo and fled inland, and not a moment too soon, as many were shot down by arrows from the Joseon ships. Yi burned the beached ships and spent the next several days searching for more prey, but none was to be found. At the cost of just 13 dead and 37 wounded in his second campaign, Yi had destroyed three Japanese squadrons, killing hundreds, if not thousands, of Japanese sailors and troops. Yi made excellent use of the tactical formations he had drilled his fleet in, particularly at Danghangpo. Elated at news of these victories, the Joseon court bestowed Yi a reward along the civil *Mungwa* track, a promotion to *Jahun Daeboo* (2nd-rank civil servant). The Joseon refugees, hiding in the mountains, took heart at seeing Yi's victorious ships sailing by, running to the shore to provide any information they had on Japanese troop movements. Yi distributed the supplies he had captured from his battles to these refugees. The number of civilians entering the safety of Yi's headquarters at Yeosu also increased. Following royal orders to assist the civilian refugees, Yi addressed issues of food supply and the starving refugees crowding around his base by resettling 200 families to form farming villages on Tolsan Island after carefully identifying it as a place that was both arable and within the operation zone of the Jeolla Left Navy.

THE THIRD CAMPAIGN: HANSANDO AND ANGOLPO

It took a long time for word that an element of the Joseon navy was still fighting and wreaking havoc to reach Hideyoshi. After hearing about Okpo in the sixth month, Hideyoshi sent orders to his chief field commander, Ukita Hideie, to, among other things, capture Jeolla Province, find and destroy the remnants of the Joseon navy and expedite the breakthrough to the western coast. To defeat Yi, Hideyoshi assembled a dedicated task force of his most skilled naval commanders. On 14d 6m, Wakizaka, Kuki and Kato arrived in Busan and strategized. Their plan was simple – to find Yi, give battle and overwhelm him with their numerically superior force. Morale in the Japanese camp was high. One Korean prisoner who witnessed the assembly of Japanese troops recounted, 'I heard them say in angry voices that the Korean sailors from Jeolla Province had burned their boats and cut off the heads of their comrades. Then I saw them wave swords and yell, as if to march toward that province immediately.' However, the combined Japanese fleet quickly ran into issues of command and control. Wakizaka finished his preparations before Kuki and Kato, and left Gimhae for Geoje Island on the 6d 7m. According to the Wakizaka family records, he advanced ahead by himself so that he would not have to share the glory of victory.

Yi received orders to attack once more, based on information that a large Japanese fleet was gathering at Busan. After conducting joint-fleet exercises with Yi Eok-gi for two days starting on 4d 7m, the two set sail with 51 ships (including two or three geobukseon) on 6d 7m, and united with Won Gyun's seven ships at Noryang. On the night of the following day, a shepherd named Kim Cheon-son who had been hiding in the mountains spotted the passing Joseon fleet and came down from his hiding spot with valuable information – he had counted 70 Japanese ships anchored around Gyeongnaeryang and Geoje Island at around 1400hrs. The Joseon generals held a council of war. Won Gyun advocated for an immediate attack through the Gyeongnaeryang Strait, confident that Joseon firepower would win the day. Yi pointed out that the strait was narrow and surrounded by reefs, making any attack up the strait by the heavy Joseon ships difficult. Won Gyun's frontal attack could give them a victory, but Yi sought annihilation. Knowing that the Japanese sailors could just flee to shore and pillage their way back to Busan, Yi proposed that they lure Wakizaka out of the strait and crush him in open water where there was no escape, save for the deserted islands of Hwado and Hansando.

On the morning of the 8th, Yi sailed to Gyeongnaeryang. He pursued a Japanese vanguard of two ships to the point where he could see the rest of Wakizaka's fleet beyond the strait, anchored in a long row. In all, Wakizaka had with him 73 ships – 36 large, 24 medium and 13 small. Kato and Kuki had yet to fully consolidate their fleets, and their ships were trickling into the assembly points some distance behind Wakizaka's. Yi tasked Eo Yeong-dam with leading a vanguard of five ships from the Jeolla Left Navy fleet into the strait to lure Wakizaka out. The bulk of the Joseon fleet remained under Yi's command in front of the strait. Yi positioned his ambush forces carefully, making sure they were hidden from the view of any ship emerging from the strait: on the left, Yi Eok-gi took the Jeolla Right Navy to Tongyeong bay, while on the right, Won Gyun's squadron took up a similar position at Hwado Island.

Coming into view of the Japanese fleet, Eo's vanguard seized their attention by firing a broadside, and Wakizaka's men immediately began to fire their arquebuses in response. This firefight occurred for about 30 minutes.

A display of Joseon small arms and the armour-piercing flechettes that would have been fired from them. The hand cannons from top to bottom are: *samchongtong* (predecessor to the Seungja chongtong), *samanchong* (triple-barrelled gun) and a Seungja chongtong. Before the Seungja chongtong was invented, Joseon small arms typically only fired flechettes, with different types of hand cannons firing exclusively either clusters of anti-personnel flechettes or larger armour-piercing flechettes. The Seungja chongtong was unique from its predecessors in that it could fire buckshot in addition to larger flechettes, combining the individual abilities of its multiple predecessors into one gun. (Photograph by Yuhan Kim, from the Korea National Science Museum)

The *sajogu* was a large four-pronged grappling hook used by the Joseon navy, said to have been invented by Admiral Yi. Attached to a chain, it would have been difficult to throw at any great distance, but just as difficult to remove once it latched onto a victim ship. It was used by Joseon crews to board crippled Japanese vessels. The sajogu also had a possible secondary use of fishing out debris and corpses (as is often mentioned in Yi's diary). Displayed alongside it is a bigyeokjincheonroe, with the triangular iron shards that would have filled it. (Photograph by Kim Min-su, Okpo Battle Memorial Park)

When Eo retreated back into the strait, Wakizaka launched his fleet in pursuit. In their haste to catch Eo, Wakizaka's fleet sailed out in an ad hoc column, rather than a battle formation, with a squadron of atakebune leading the way. Wakizaka was confident in the abilities of his men, and likely underestimated the Joseon navy's fighting capabilities given his prior experience at the battle of Yongin. However, Wakizaka was no fool in this situation. He was likely aware of the possibility of an ambush at the mouth of the Gyeongnaeryang, balking when he saaw Yi's fleet come into view. But as Eo's vanguard joined Yi's ships, the entire fleet retreated together. Encouraged by the flight of the Joseon fleet and seeing no ambush as he exited the strait, Wakizaka let out a sigh of relief and signalled to his fleet to press ahead at full speed, knowing that in time his faster ships would overtake and board the Joseon ships. The Joseon crews rowed madly to escape the Japanese ships, which were fast closing in on them. Yi allowed the chase to continue for several kilometres, even as the Japanese nipped at his heels.

When the chase reached the west of Hwado Island, Yi gave the signal. As drums beat and flags were raised, sails folded for battle and cannons rolled out, the mass of Joseon ships that had been seemingly fleeing pell-mell now peeled off in disciplined order to form a giant hagik-jin. When Yi's ships had completed their sudden redeployment, their left and right extended forwards, eveloping Wakizaka's flanks. Disordered from the pursuit and caught in a column, Wakizaka's men scrambled to respond to the sudden turn of events, but Yi afforded them little opportunity to do so. A thunderous broadside rippled across the entire arc of the hagik-jin, sending a mass of shot, arrows and janggunjeon hurtling towards the atakebune squadron at the head of the column and reducing it to splinters. As Wakizaka's ships staggered forwards under withering fire, Yi put the next part of his plan into motion. Yi Eok-gi and Won Gyun's previously hidden squadrons sailed forth to hammer the Japanese flank and rear with cannon fire. Wakizaka was now surrounded.

The battle of Hansando, 8d 7m

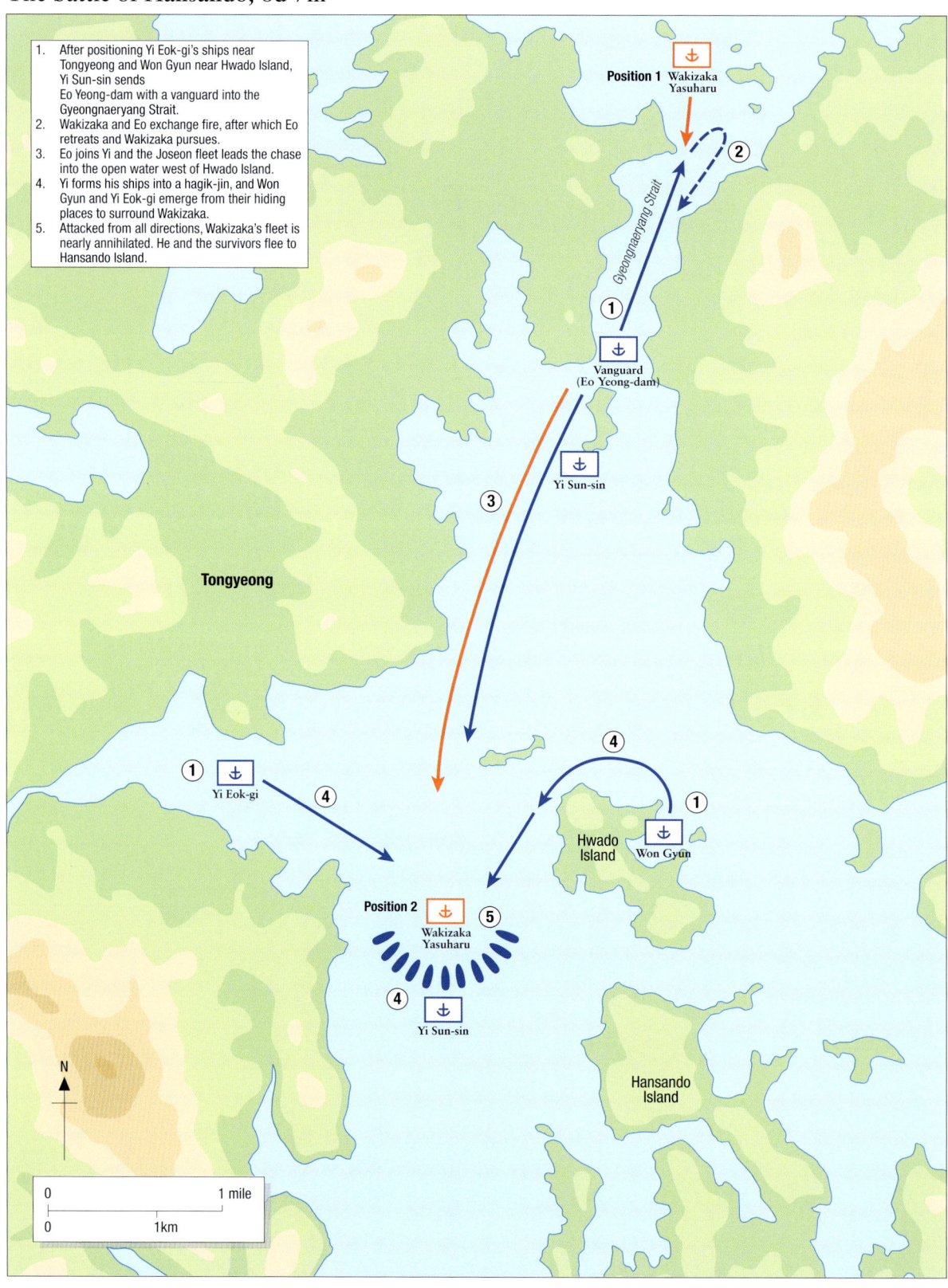

Yi roared the order to charge, and Joseon ships closed the distance with a cacophony of drums and shouts, crews waving their battle flags. They tore through the disordered Japanese fleet, firing their cannons as they went without regard for the risk of being boarded. Yi's ships targeted the atakebune in particular. Yi writes:

> Our ships dashed forward with the roar of the Hyeonja, Jija, and Cheonja cannons, breaking the enemy vessels into pieces. The other enemy vessels, stricken with terror, scattered and fled in all directions in great confusion. Our officers and men and local officials on board shouted 'Victory!' and darted at flying speed, vying with one another, as they rained down arrows and bullets like a hailstorm, burning the enemy vessels and slaughtering his warriors completely.

Kwon Jun was the first into the fray, singling out an atakebune as his prey and racing his panokseon ahead to pour fire into it. Kwon and his marines boarded the crippled ship and slashed a bloody path across the deck, fighting their way to the ship's samurai captain, who Kwon killed. Joseon gunners cleared the decks of Japanese ships with bigyeokjincheonroe or shingijeons before Joseon marines boarded them to take heads as trophies. Eo Yeong-dam boarded an atakebune and mortally wounded its captain with an arrow. For the Japanese who leapt from their shattered vessels, there was no escape, as Yi had planned, and most drowned. Wakizaka's atakebune was set on fire and boarded. With his men lying wounded, burning or drowning all around him, and his own ship crippled, Wakizaka gave the order to abandon ship. He transferred to a nearby boat and made for shore, closely pursued by Joseon ships. The *Wakizaka-ki* family history recounts:

This stylized painting of the battle of Hansando captures the chaos of the second phase of the battle, as Joseon ships attack Wakizaka's fleet at close range. (Courtesy of the Jeseungdang)

Due to the situation, Yasuharu [Wakizaka] transferred to a sekibune. While the boat was agile and sturdy, his [Wakizaka's] life was threatened when his armour was hit by an arrow. The enemy ships pursued, shooting fire-arrows, and Yasuharu retreated towards Gimhae. Some 200 men barely managed to survive the clutches of the enemy, fleeing 5.5km to a small island [Hansando], but when we landed, the panokseons had followed and set fire to our ship. The ship had been captained by a man named Manabe Samonojo, who felt that because his ship had been burned, he did not have the honour to face his comrades again, so he committed seppuku and died.

Wakizaka was joined there by more survivors, some 400 in all. Yi ordered Won Gyun to blockade Hansando and let Wakizaka and his men starve to death on the desolate island.

Yi's men were too exhausted to mount a pursuit, so the battle ended where their ships stood. In all, the Japanese lost 47 ships sunk and 12 damaged, amounting to several thousand casualties, including two of Wakizaka's lieutenants, Wakizaka Sahyoe and Watanabe Shichiemon, killed in action. Only one large ship, seven medium ships and six small ships escaped the encirclement, only by the fortune of falling behind in the initial pursuit. The Jeolla Right Navy and Gyeongsang Right Navy accounted for the destruction of 42 ships (20 large, 17 medium, five small), the rest, 15 atakebune and two small ships, were sunk by Yi's men. Yi's losses for the battle of Hansando alone are not known, but it totalled just 19 dead and 114 wounded for the actions at Hansando and Angolpo combined. Won Gyun and Yi Eok-gi's losses are not known, but they could not have been great. To Yi's joy, his men rescued a number of Joseon prisoners when they boarded the Japanese ships. Yi was liberal with his praise in the post-battle report, making a detailed account of how many heads each of his officers had taken, and who had contributed in other ways, noting how Yi Sun-sin (M) did not take as many heads as the others 'because he was more interested in shooting down the living than

A display of Joseon arrows. The cylinders attached to two of the arrows are gunpowder charges that would be lit before shooting and then explode after reaching their target. The bottommost arrow is a standard fire-arrow with flammable material wrapped around the front. As it was quite difficult to sink a ship with cannon alone, the Joseon navy generally used artillery to cripple ships and finished them off with incendiaries. The third from the bottom is a *pyeonjeon* with its accompanying bamboo arrow guide. The pyeonjeon was a smaller arrow that would be shot from a regular bow using the arrow guide. This allowed for greater range and velocity than a normal arrow. (Photograph by Kim Min-su, Okpo Battle Memorial Park)

The battle of Hansando, in a painting at the War Memorial of Korea. In the foreground is a smaller hyeopseon packed with archers, while the focal point is Yi's panokseon and its combat crew. In the background are geobukseon and panokseon, depicted with a variety of command pavilions. While the painting depicts a geobukseon ramming an atakebune, in all likelihood the geobukseon was not used for ramming attacks. (From the War Memorial of Korea)

in cutting the heads of the dead. Then he chased and destroyed two more enemy vessels, burning them completely.'

Kuki and Kato were greatly unnerved at seeing the broken remnants of Wakizaka's fleet stream through the Gyeongnaeryang Strait. How could it be that 73 ships had left just a few hours ago and only 14 returned? With just 42 ships between them (21 large, 15 medium and six small), they retreated to Angolpo bay. But Yi was not long in following them, arriving there on the morning of the 10th after taking a day to rest. Kuki and Kato had chosen an excellent defensive position and were well prepared for Yi's attack. They spaced out their ships to minimize the effects of the Joseon artillery and set up their own batteries on land. Additionally, the entrance to the area was very narrow and the heavy-drafted Joseon ships could only sail in when the tide was high between 0500hrs and 0700hrs, and 1700hrs and 1900hrs. As Angolpo was just around 30km from Busan, Yi left a flotilla at Gadeok Island at the mouth of the entrance to Angolpo and sailed the rest of his fleet through the strait in single file at 0500hrs. Yi performed a feigned retreat, hoping the Japanese would pursue him, but Kuki and Kato knew better than to fall for Yi's trap as Wakizaka had. At least in Angolpo bay, they could flee to land if they were attacked.

The *jingasa* was the representative headgear of the Japanese ashigaru. Made of hardened leather and iron, its conical shape helped deflect attacks, and it could also be used as a cooking pot by its wearer. This particular example was used by troops of the Kuki clan. (From the Ikunoshin Kadono Memorial Museum in Toba City, Japan)

A surviving example of *Yokohagi okegawa do* (horizontally riveted cuirass) armour of an ashigaru of the Kuki clan, displayed at the Toba City History Museum. Made of iron plates, the Yokohagi armour style was among the most common in 16th-century Japan. The seven red circles represent the 'Shichiyoumon', one of the symbols used by Kuki Yoshitaka as his crest. (From the Ikunoshin Kadono Memorial Museum in Toba City, Japan)

Rather than try to rush the Japanese fleet head on, Yi opted for an attritional battle that would maximize his advantage in firepower. He sent his ships in two at a time, to fire off their heavy guns from outside of the range of the land batteries, then sail back to switch out with another pair.

Yi likely used this unusual deployment to maintain a substantial reserve and prevent being trapped in the bay by a Japanese fleet from Busan and to make sure his ships were never unloaded when they sailed against the Japanese. If there was a moment where a panokseon was caught reloading its guns, there was a chance that the Japanese could sally out and swarm it. This naval caracole went on for two gruelling hours. The Joseon ships made special use of their anti-ship large wooden arrows, and the Japanese fought tenaciously, firing with what weapons they had and working frantically to plug holes and put out fires. At 0700hrs, Yi ordered his ships to retreat as the high tide ebbed. Kuki and Kato quickly set to work repairing their ships and tending to their wounded, but ten hours later, with the resurgence of the high tide, the Joseon fleet emerged once more. Yi performed the same methodical operation he had done that morning – a Japanese naval report writes, 'While shooting [various types of large arrows], they charged in turns until 6 pm… These stone fire-arrows were 5 feet 6 inches [about 117.6cm] long and made of solid wood… Also, the tips of the daejanggunjeon were made of iron and firmly attached in a round shape. With these large arrows, they would come within five kan [1 kan is about 1.25m] or three kan and shoot…' At some point, the land batteries must have been silenced, for the Joseon ships closed in until they were at point-blank range, the geobukseon leading the way. The massive *Nihon Maru* made for an especially tempting target, and Japanese accounts relate how the thick triple-layered curtains provided effective protection against Joseon arrows, which tore through just the first two layers. To stop fire-arrows, its crew had covered the hull with wet bags of straw and blankets and soaked them continuously. *Nihon Maru* was raked with close-range cannon fire, tearing 3ft-wide gashes into its hull, but the crew was well prepared and quickly boarded up the damage and bailed out water.

The battle of Angolpo, 10d 7m

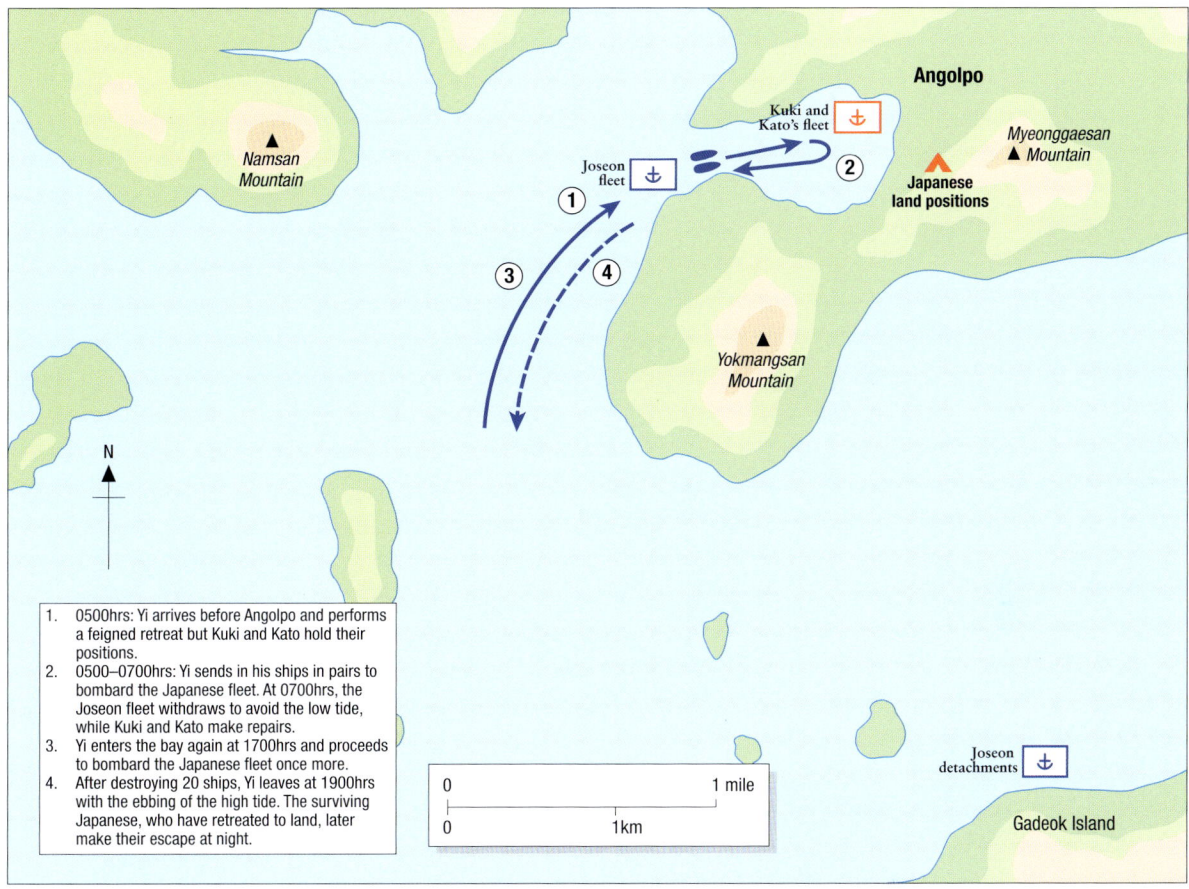

1. 0500hrs: Yi arrives before Angolpo and performs a feigned retreat but Kuki and Kato hold their positions.
2. 0500–0700hrs: Yi sends in his ships in pairs to bombard the Japanese fleet. At 0700hrs, the Joseon fleet withdraws to avoid the low tide, while Kuki and Kato make repairs.
3. Yi enters the bay again at 1700hrs and proceeds to bombard the Japanese fleet once more.
4. After destroying 20 ships, Yi leaves at 1900hrs with the ebbing of the high tide. The surviving Japanese, who have retreated to land, later make their escape at night.

When it came time to close the action at 1900hrs with the ebbing of the tides, Yi ultimately decided not to burn all the Japanese ships, noting that:

> however, we were unable to capture and slaughter all the defeated Japanese who escaped to land. At that time there was a large number of civilians hiding in the mountains nearby. If we burned all the Japanese boats, the surviving Japanese, cut off from escape by sea, would kill the refugees wantonly, so leaving a few Japanese boats intact, we pulled out about one li (0.3 miles) out to sea to pass the night.

When the Joseon fleet had long sailed away, the surviving Japanese emerged from the woods and hills and ventured carefully back to their ships. Taking advantage of nightfall, Kuki and Kato took their surviving 22 ships and sailed out of Angolpo back to Busan. To Kuki's astonishment, *Nihon Maru* had miraculously withstood the assault and was still seaworthy thanks to the efforts of the crew. Yi hoped to finish off Kuki and Kato and spent most of the 11th dispatching reconnaissance parties and sailing around different ports around Busan, hunting for more prey. Finding nothing except that the Japanese ships in the area had fled after hearing cannon fire at Angolpo, Yi turned his ships back.

Overall, the Japanese lost 20 ships and hundreds of men. Yi reported that, 'We searched the place where the battle had taken place the day before and found that the dead Japanese had been gathered in 12 places and burnt.

BATTLE OF ANGOLPO, 10D 7M 1592 (PP. 62–63)

Yi followed up on his victory at Hansando by attacking Kuki Yoshitaka and Kato Yoshiaki's combined fleet at Angolpo harbour. Unable to lure the Japanese ships out to open water or engage in the shallow bay, Yi sends in his panokseon in rotations of pairs **(1)** to bombard the Japanese ships with his long-range Cheonja cannons. Here, Japanese arquebusiers **(2)** on board a sekibune return fire with small arms against the artillery barrage of the Joseon fleet. Under heavy fire, they nonetheless manage to form a rudimentary firing line, but the Joseon ships are barely within effective range. Their efforts are aided by a samurai and his ashigaru loader, who prepare to fire an Ozutsu teppo **(3)**, an oversized arquebus. To the left, another sekibune **(4)** is raked with fire and beginning to sink, and its surviving crew and wounded are boarding a kobaya to transfer to another ship. To the right **(5)**, *Nihon Maru*, its hull draped with thick blanket rolls as makeshift armour, turns into the line of fire to try and shield the smaller ships. Topped with a three-level pagoda, *Nihon Maru* was a giant atakebune (O-atakebune) built in 1592 and was the pride of Hideyoshi's fleet. Fittingly, it was Kuki's flagship for the invasion of Korea. Much to Hideyoshi's joy, the ship survived the battle and served as a template for mid-war Japanese ship designs. Kuki took with him a unique souvenir for his troubles, a daejanggunjeon embedded in the hull of *Nihon Maru*. It was probably a helpful visual aid for Kuki when explaining the circumstances of his defeat to Hideyoshi, and was passed down in his family. Today it remains the only surviving example of such a projectile from the Imjin War.

Their bones and limbs were scattered about, and the ground inside and outside the port was covered in blood, and as you can see here and there, the number of casualties among the bandits was incalculable.'

On the way back to his base, Yi passed by Hansando Island, where Wakizaka and his men were 'sitting dazed on the shore, lame, and having gone hungry for many days'. As he was running low on food and hearing that the Japanese were attacking Jeolla, Yi tasked Won Gyun with orders to remain and work with local militias to finish off the 400 survivors (or 200, according to the Wakizaka family record). These unfortunate men languished on the island, subsiding on nothing but the seaweed that washed up on shore and pine needles they picked off the trees. They were kept from leaving by Won's squadron, which hovered offshore, waiting for the Japanese to starve to death before closing in like vultures. After nearly two weeks of being marooned, an opportunity presented itself when Won Gyun lifted his blockade and retreated after receiving a false report of a Japanese rescue fleet. Wakizaka tried to launch some wooden rafts his men had been building, but the panokseon returned to fire at the Japanese on the beach, killing ten men. However, when they left, Wakizaka and his surviving men used the rafts to escape to Geoje Island at last. Yi commented, 'In this way, the fish jumped out of the cooking pot, to our great indignation.'

This picture of two atakebune is part of a larger screen depicting the entire Hizen-Nagoya Castle. It has been speculated that one of the two ships is *Nihon Maru*, though it is unknown which one exactly. (From the Saga Prefectural Nagoya Castle Museum)

Meanwhile on land, Kobayakawa Takakage's 6th Division was attempting to invade Jeolla Province in accordance with Hideyoshi's directives. In what is known as the Geumsan campaign, the Japanese 6th Division launched a two-pronged attack into Jeolla. The southern arm, led by the unlucky commander Ankokouji Ekei, was turned back by Righteous Army guerrillas. Kobayakawa won at the hard-fought battle of Kumsan, then pressed on to defeat another Korean force at Ungchi. But an effective Joseon rearguard prevented Kobayakawa from exploiting his victories. At the same time as the battle of Hansando, another element of the 6th Division had been defeated at the battle of Ichi by Marshal Kwon Yul and General Hwang Jin, dashing Japanese hopes of ending the Joseon naval threat by taking Yi's bases by land.

Yi had great reason to be satisfied with his victories. Capitalizing on Wakizaka's overconfidence, he had defeated the Japanese fleet in detail. Tactically, the battle of Hansando was one of the few battles in history to defy von Moltke's mantra that 'No plan survives contact with the enemy.' Through excellent use of terrain to conceal his flanking units and luring the Japanese fleet into a ground of his choosing, Yi turned victory into annihilation. The destruction of the Japanese task force at Hansando and Angolpo meant that Yi had supremacy over the waters of Korea for the moment. Yi was actually quite concerned that the Japanese would rally and attack Yeosu, so kept his men on high alert. However, he need not have worried, for upon hearing of the defeats, Hideyoshi ordered all his ships to avoid confrontation with the Joseon navy and confined them to port. When one of Yi's officers, Yi Chung, arrived at the Joseon court bearing news of the victories, the Seonjo Sillok (Joseon court records) notes, 'everyone in the Haengjo [temporary wartime palace established if the main palace was lost] was overjoyed and there was no one who did not celebrate'. High praise was heaped on the victors, and over many meetings, the Joseon court discussed how to reward the victorious admiral and his captains.

After the death of Sin Rip at Chungju, Kwon Yul rose to become Joseon's foremost commander on land. Credited with two great victories at Ichi and Hanegju, he was for want of more victories in the latter half of the war as he attempted to dislodge the Japanese from their *wajo* strongholds. Known to be a stern disciplinarian, he executed fleeing soldiers in battle to hold the line, and in spite of his impossible victory at Hanegju, considered Ichi to be his greatest triumph for its greater strategic impact. (From the War Memorial of Korea)

THE FOURTH CAMPAIGN: BUSAN

By the eighth month of 1592, the initial Japanese advance had turned into a gruelling war of attrition. Guerrilla bands were beginning to organize and pose a serious threat to Japanese garrisons and supply lines in Gyeongsang Province. Ming China had intervened in the war as well (Joseon was a client state of the Ming), and dispatched an army in the sixth month. There were reports that the Japanese were fleeing south, including one by a Gyeongsang Province official that stated that the Japanese 'are hiding during the day and marching only at night, coming down to Yangsan and Gimhae River one after another. Judging from the fact that they are fully loaded with luggage, their movements are clearly intended to escape.' A captured Japanese soldier testified, 'During the sixth and seventh moons the Japanese senior officers sent messengers to bring their wives by cargo

A Japanese drawing of Kuki Yoshitaka's fleet anchored at Busan. A wide variety of ships are shown, from single-decked kobaya or sekibune to multi-tiered sekibune and atakebune. The ship in the centre is quite possibly *Nihon Maru*. The front line of ships is chained together, likely to protect the more valuable heavy vessels in the centre. Perhaps the most striking element of the drawing is the way it depicts the large curtains that were draped all across the sides of the Japanese ships, as so often mentioned in Yi's reports. (東京大学駒場図書館 Komaba Library, The University of Tokyo, Japan)

boats. Therefore they did not like to go out to the battlefields, but retired into deep mountain valleys. As the Koreans killed the Japanese in large numbers, endangering them, they wished to go home. I was captured as I was preparing to return to my country.' Such news led Yi to incorrectly believe that the Japanese were on the verge of abandoning Korea. The Japanese movements in Gyeongsang were either movements of local units not reflective of the strategic situation of the entire Japanese army or units being sent south from the central divisions by Ukita Hideie to deal with the increasing guerrilla threat. Determined to strike the Japanese line of retreat, Yi planned for another offensive and called for the Jeolla Right and Gyeongsang Left navies to join him.

On 24d 8m, Yi and Yi Eok-gi set sail. They met Won Gyun's fleet the next day at Dangpo, and continued to sail east. The combined Joseon armada was impressive. Yi and his men had been hard at work in the past months constructing new ships. The two Jeolla navies totalled 74 panokseon and three geobukseon, and 94 hyeopseon. Won Gyun had ten panokseon and hyeopseon in total. All of this amounted to over 15,000 crew and over 1,000 cannons. On the 28th, Yi received intelligence from a refugee that the Japanese ships had been massing on the Nakdong River near Gimhae for several days and were likely planning to escape. If Yi was going to attack Busan, then he could not run the risk of having any Japanese ships in the Nakdong emerge to attack his rear. Yi positioned his fleet in ambush positions around Gadeok Island and dispatched a scout ship up the Nakdong River towards Yangsan. It returned at 1700hrs, having sighted nothing other than four small ships. Yi decided not to pursue and rested his troops. Trying again the next day (29th), Yi had better luck and encountered four large and two small ships emerging from the mouth of the Nakdong at Janglimpo. Seeing the Japanese immediately abandon ship at the sight of the Joseon navy, Yi settled for burning the abandoned ships. Furthermore, the Nakdong delta was too narrow for the

The fourth campaign, 24d 8m–1d 9m

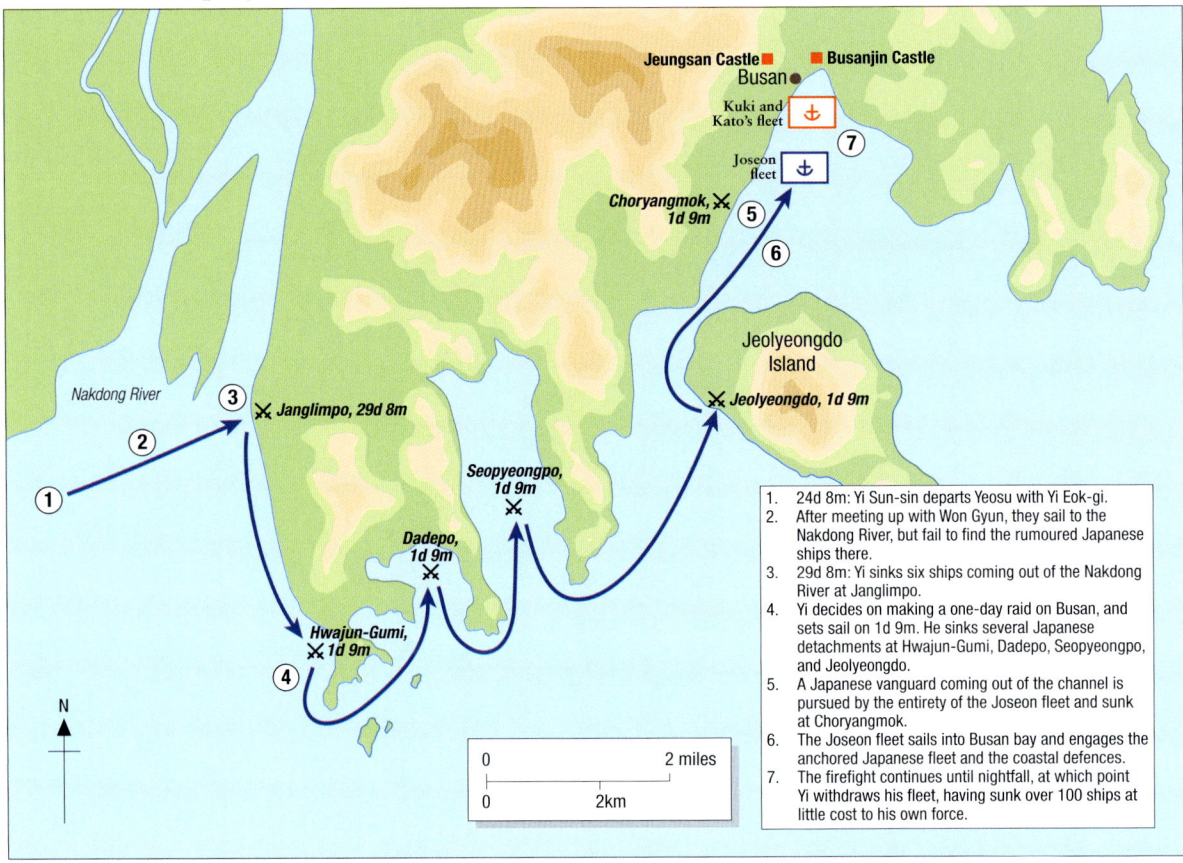

panokseon to sail effectively, so Yi could only wait outside at the mouth to intercept ships as they left. As such, Yi and his generals decided to continue onwards to Busan rather than further investigate the rumoured squadrons at Yangsan. But Gadeok Island was the last safe harbour available to Yi, where he could be sure that there were no Japanese ships in the vicinity. The waters between Gadeok Island and Busan were rough and windy, and the coastal inlets were far too close to the Japanese base. Any attack on Busan would have to be made from Gadeok Island in a single day, and with not enough daylight left, Yi returned his ships to north of Gadeok Island to spend the night.

The next day, 1d 9m, the Joseon fleet sailed towards Busan. On the way, they caught and destroyed several more isolated Japanese units – five ships at Hwajun-Gumi, eight at Dadepo, nine at Seopyeongpo and two at Jeolyeongdo Island (Namhang-dong). Then, Yi's scout ships reported that they had spotted the main Japanese concentration – some 500 ships were anchored at Busan. The entrance to Busan harbour from the west was a narrow channel between the mainland and Jeolyeongdo Island. When four atakebune were seen emerging from the channel, Yi conferred with his officers, saying 'If we do not attack now with the strength at our disposal and turn back, the enemy will undoubtedly look down on us.' Forming their ships into a single file to navigate the channel, Yi and Yi Eok-gi yelled 'Do or die!' and directed the Joseon fleet towards Busan. Lee Eon-ryang led the geobukseon squadron, Jeong Un commanded the right flank, Shin Ho the left, followed by Kwon Jun and Yi Sun-sin (M). At the sight of an endless stream of Joseon warships, the crew of the four atakebune abandoned their ships at Choryangmok and swam for shore.

In Busan harbour were 470 ships, the combined fleets of Todo Takatora, Wakizaka Yasuharu, Kato Yoshiaki and Kuki Yoshitaka. In response to the defeat at Hansando, Hideyoshi had dispatched Todo Takatora with new orders dictating a change in naval strategy. No longer was the Japanese navy to fight Yi at sea; it would instead stay in port to avoid total defeat. Todo brought with him more than just orders – he also had reinforcements, comprising new squadrons of atakebune from Kyushu, Chugoku and Shikoku. Hideyoshi had also ordered the construction of more durable and larger atakebune to counter the firepower of the panokseon, but these had yet to take to the seas. Japanese military personnel at Busan numbered at least 18,000 – some 10,000 soldiers and 8,000 sailors (likely more) – and the garrison was commanded by Toyotomi (Hashiba) Hidekatsu, one of Hideyoshi's adopted sons. (He is often confused with Oda Nobunaga's fourth son and also Hideyoshi's adopted son, who was also named Hashiba Hidekatsu [1567–86].) Anticipating that the Joseon navy would attack Busan at some point, Ishida Mitsunari, one of three 'commissioners' appointed by Hideyoshi to be part of the invasion force's chief of staff, had pored through the reports of the naval defeats from his office in Hanyang and dictated a thorough defensive plan for the daimyo at Busan:

1. Establish watchtowers along the Joseon navy's expected paths to Busan. If the Joseon fleet is spotted moving to Busan, all ships will concentrate at Busan.
2. Build up and reinforce the port breakwater.
3. Obtain as many Joseon cannons as possible and learn how to use them.
4. Build as many catapults as possible and place them in appropriate locations.
5. Deploy troops to areas where the enemy may disembark troops.
6. Concentrate fire against the turtle ships and the enemy flagship.
7. The ship crews should be trained and organized into firefighting teams and sharpshooters.
8. Dig trenches in places favourable for attacking the enemy, and build new fortifications if necessary.
9. If it is confirmed that the enemy is moving to Busan, sound the alarm and maintain battle stations, even at night.
10. When the battle ends, report the results immediately, and do not leave any omissions.

The Japanese commanders at Busan had taken this advice to heart and made thorough preparations along the lines of those prescribed by Ishida. They had days of advance notice that Yi was on his way, each step he took noted by reports from the fleeing crews of the ships he sunk.

When Yi's ships emerged from the channel at 1400hrs, flags fluttering and drums beating, they found the Japanese land troops were ready to meet them, formed up in six main fortified positions, while the Japanese fleet was formed into three large groups behind the breakwater. Both sides hurled a storm of shot at each other, the Japanese firing their arquebuses,

BATTLE OF BUSAN, 1D 9M 1592 (PP. 70–71)

Upon the arrival of the Joseon fleet, the Japanese abandoned their ships and retreated to their fortifications. Fighting on land, the Japanese were able to employ their artillery against Yi's navy, which was drawn up in a long line formation. In the foreground, Yi and his flagship captains observe the battle and coordinate the different squadrons by signal flag **(1)**. Yi and his officers wear dujeonggap or *chal-gap* (lamellar). On deck, a marine prepares to fire a Seungja chongtong, loaded with a piryeong-mokjeon armour-piercing flechette **(2)**. The uniforms of the Joseon officers and crew are based on research by Gyeongnam Province and the 21st-century Yi Sun-sin Research Association. The entire battle was fought with the Koreans firing at the moored ships while simultaneously engaging in counter-battery fire **(3)**. Yi writes that his ships were ultimately able to silence the Japanese artillery, an effort that took his fleet all day. Much to the anger of Yi and his men, the Japanese had demolished the Korean government buildings there and built hundreds of earthen barracks over them – the area is today known as the Busanjinseong **(4)**.

An example of the comparative fortress doctrines of each country, the Japanese built a new citadel on the Jeungsan mountain **(5)**. At the time of the battle, the fortress itself was little more than a system of earthworks, as the finished citadel replete with stone bastions was constructed in March–August 1593. There was a large, whitewashed building that served as a central command post, surrounded by layers of earthen walls and a moat. The slopes of the mountain were covered with some 300 Japanese houses of more refined construction than the barracks, likely offices and private residences. Yi had intended for the destruction of the Japanese fleet to be immediately followed up with an amphibious assault, but seeing numerous Japanese cavalry and having none of his own, decided against it. He also wanted to launch an attack the next day, this time targeting the Japanese buildings, but decided against it on the grounds that if he did so the Japanese would retreat and wreak havoc further inland. Today the remains of the Japanese citadel encompass a community area with a sports centre, library and kindergarten.

arrows, catapults and captured Joseon cannons from their entrenchments and batteries, while the Joseon ships formed up into six hagik-jin and opened fire against the coastal positions and the anchored fleet. Yi recounts:

> When our ships came in to a close attack the enemy hordes on ships, on land, and in the mountain trenches uphill poured down upon us arrows and gunfire from six positions, and sometimes hurled cannon balls the size of a Chinese quince, or large stones as big as rice bowls which fell on our ships with thundering sounds. Undaunted, our men, braving death, dashed forward as they shot Cheonja and Jija chongtongs, and janggunjeon, piryongchajungjeon and pyeonjeon.

The Joseon ships could only sail so far due to the shallow waters. This ferocious long-range duel continued for hours, encasing Busan in smoke. One part of the Joseon fleet lay down a heavy fire on the fortifications, while another methodically sunk and burned the Japanese fleet. The civilian volunteer captain Cho Chong, serving in Kwon Jun's Suncheon squadron, distinguished himself in combat. Unfortunatley, Jeong Un was shot in the forehead and killed by a sharpshooter armed with an Ozutsu teppo. The shot reportedly tore 'through three oak shields, two bags of rice, and Jeong Un's body before entering the ship's storage room'. The Japanese were taking heavy losses, and dragged their wounded into the entrenchments. By the end of the day, some 100 Japanese ships lay at the bottom of the harbour, and countless more were damaged. At dusk, the silence over Busan harbour was deafening after the five- to six-hour-long thunderous exchange.

Yi's Jeolla Left Navy suffered just six killed and 25 injured – light casualties considering the intensity of the battle, but among them was the irreplaceable Jeong Un. Of the injured, three had been hit by arrows, the rest by gunfire. Casualties for Yi Eok-gi and Won Gyun's fleets are unknown, but were likely far less than Yi's, as Yi's men formed the vanguard and were the most hotly engaged. For the Japanese, casualties are difficult to estimate, as the units were spread out across land and sea, but were undoubtedly in the hundreds. The heavy smoke likely played a role in the ineffectiveness of Japanese fire, while the Joseon accuracy was less impeded as their targets were static.

Yi wanted to follow up on his naval attack by landing his marines and sailors to finish off the defenders, but he observed numerous Japanese cavalry units. Yi had no cavalry of his own, his men were exhausted and night was coming, so Yi decided to order the fleet back to Gadeok Island. He contemplated carrying out his amphibious assault the following day with the objective of raiding the Japanese barracks and burning them down. However, realizing that this would incentivize the Japanese to maraud inland for supplies, Yi decided against it and resolved to finish what he had started when the Japanese were forced into the sea by a major offensive on land. Additionally, he was running low on gunpowder and food, and the waves had become

Joseon troops typically used two types of shields – *paengbae* (round) or *jangbangpae* (rectangular). This jangbangpae, standing at around 5ft, is strikingly painted with a dragon's face. It is made of wood and reinforced leather. Paengbae were used in close combat, while the large and unwieldy jangbangpae served as pavises in stationary defence against projectiles. Such shields were used on panokseon to defend the unprotected command pavilion and mounted on the battlements of the ship. (From the collection of the National Museum of Korea, accessible at https://www.emuseum.go.kr/)

rougher, making any renewed assault more unpredictable. Satisfied with the damage done, Yi ordered the united fleet to disband for the time being, as he sailed back triumphantly to Yeosu. On 17d 9m, Yi dispatched one of his officers, Song Yo-chong, to carry his campaign report to King Seonjo. Song had decorated himself highly at Busan and the battles before it, and Yi was determined to reward this worthy subordinate by granting him an audience with King Seonjo. With the Joseon court in exile, it was no easy task for Song to locate them. He had to move at night to avoid Japanese troops, even sneaking past their encampments, before he finally reached the court. King Seonjo interviewed him personally, and after commending his hard work, promoted Song to fill Jeong Un's former position as Nokdo Port Captain.

While Yi had not captured Busan nor sunk the entire Japanese fleet, the attack on their main base of operations greatly unnerved the Japanese expeditionary force. The battle of Busan demonstrated that their supply line, and most importantly for the troops, their way back home, was under constant threat of attack. Perhaps suffering from exhaustion and stress after the battle, Toyotomi Hidekatsu fell ill not long after the battle and died at Geoje Island on 14d 10m. Another consequence of the battle of Busan was that it may have contributed to Toyotomi Hideyoshi deciding not to cross the sea to personally command the expeditionary force. It appears that he had plans to do so in the fifth month of 1592, but postponed his plans to the third month of 1593 and continued to push it back, ultimately never setting foot in Korea.

THE FIFTH CAMPAIGN: UNGPO

In 1593, the strategic situation was looking much less auspicious for Hideyoshi. On sea, Yi had wreaked havoc and threatened the lifeline of the invasion force. On land, Joseon forces scored an important victory at the first siege of Jinju, successfully defending a key fortress that safeguarded one of the main roads to Jeolla. A successful Ming–Joseon counterattack pushed Konishi Yukinaga's troops out of Pyongyang, forcing them to fall back to the Imjin River. The cold Korean winter and various diseases such as beri-beri and cholera were beginning to take a toll on Hideyoshi's exhausted troops.

Yi, too, was not immune from problems and in late 1592 was preoccupied with manpower shortages. The conscription of soldiers, first by the regular army, which had been trounced at Yongin, then by the Righteous Army guerrillas, left Yi with the last pick of troops. Deserters from Yi's navy often ran to these other organizations, where they were subject to less discipline and rigour. An 11d 1m report noted that Yi had 5,000 men, Yi Eok-gi had 10,000 and that there were another 10,000 scattered in various garrisons. Yi was further constrained by a royal order that forbade him from recruiting substitutes from the families of deserters. In addition to trying to fill his ships with the minimum 130 crew, Yi lamented that in some garrison posts as much as 70 per cent of the garrison was dead or missing.

Between his campaigns and supplying regular army and guerrilla units, Yi had also completely exhausted his powder supply. One of his officers, Yi Pong-su, managed to produce 1,000 pounds of saltpetre, but lacking sulphur, Yi requested 100 pounds from the government. Yi took the last few months of 1592 to bolster not just his navy, but the forces in Jeolla Province as a whole, recruiting garrison troops and organizing Righteous Army guerrillas.

Yi's manpower and supply problems were partly solved by a particularly intelligent government order that requested that Yi and Won Gyun continue to look after civilian refugees and resettle them in farming communities so that they would not starve, and conscript able-bodied refugees into their forces.

The Japanese fleet had paid the price of neglect in 1592, and, rudely shaken awake to his fleet's vital role in keeping the tenuous supply line to Tsushima alive, Hideyoshi resolved to give naval matters closer personal attention in the new year. By the second month of 1593, the Japanese had rebuilt their fleet to 500 warships at Busan, and established a forward base at Ungpo with a force of 115 ships under Kuki, Kato and Wakizaka to guard the western approach to Busan. Ungpo was a well-sited location. The bay was some 1.5km long, and while 600m wide, just 200m of the channel was deep enough to be usable for a panokseon. The bay entrance was flanked by the Namsan and Baekseoksan mountains, which the Japanese built fortifications on. The Joseon Castle on Namsan was rebuilt into a Japanese-style fortress standing 180m above sea level, one that Jesuit missionary Gregorio Cespedes would note at the end of 1593 as 'an impregnable fortress with surprisingly large defensive facilities that will be completed soon'. Today it is known as the Ungcheon Japanese castle – though little is left but the ruins of its stone foundations. Behind Ungpo bay was the town of Ungcheon, where the Japanese quartered their troops.

To capitalize on the victory at Pyongyang and believing that the Japanese army would abandon the campaign, King Seonjo sent orders to Yi on 25d and 29d 1m 1593 to intercept the Japanese navy's anticipated retreat out of Korea and destroy the evacuees at sea. Yi sent word for Yi Eok-gi and Won Gyun to meet him at Gyeongnaeryang on 7d 2m, and gave orders to the squadrons of the Jeolla Left Navy to assemble at Yeosu from their regional stations by 2d 2m. His ships trickled in and by the 3rd, most of the fleet had assembled, except for Boseong magistrate Kim Deuk-gwang's squadron. Yi decided to wait for Kim, but he could not have known that the decision would cost him days. That night, a raging storm rocked the anchored ships, and it was with only great effort that the sailors managed to stabilize their ships. On the 4th, the storm was so severe that it destroyed about 9ft of the castle wall at Yeosu, forcing Yi to do his paperwork at the base guesthouse. The storm let up for a moment, but from 1800hrs and the rest of the night, the rain began again. On the 5th, Yi was surprised to find that Kim Deuk-gwang arrived at Yeosu by horse and without his squadron, which was still in harbour due to the inclement weather. Were it not for Kim's delay, the fleet could have left harbour before the storm hit. Yi had Kim disciplined, or rather, one of his captains, as it was common practice in the Joseon military at the time to punish a subordinate for the sins of their superior.

On the 6th, Yi set sail at last, and Won Gyun joined the fleet at Gyeongnaeryang on the 7th, but Yi Eok-gi was nowhere to be found. Upset, Won Gyun threatened to leave first with his ships on the morning of the 8th, but Yi Eok-gi arrived by noon, having been delayed by the storms that harried his ships in the long journey from his base. United at last, the combined fleet arrived before Ungpo on the 10th, and established a base of operations on

This iron Joseon helmet was made in the same style as the dujeonggap armour, with iron or leather scales riveted into the three flaps guarding the cheeks and back of the head. Joseon troops wore a variety of protective headgear in the Imjin War, ranging from stiffened felt hats used in peacetime (*jeollip*) to iron kettle helmets. (From the collection of the National Museum of Korea, accessible at https://www.emuseum.go.kr/)

Gadeok Island. Finding the Japanese position well defended and difficult to access, Yi attempted to lure out the Japanese squadrons hidden deep in the bay by sending in patrols. For several days, the Joseon fleet hovered at the entrance of the bay, hoping for battle, but the Japanese knew better and refused to take the bait, only sending out kobaya, which retreated with ease when pursued. Unable to engage the Japanese fleet, the Joseon captains settled for trading fire with the Japanese entrenchments and batteries on the mountainsides. Twice a day, several panokseon 'darted forward while shooting cannon balls and arrows like thunder and lightning', while the Japanese 'rained gunfire toward us in a haughty manner'. But they could not progress deeper into the bay, not knowing what the Japanese had in store for them at Ungpo.

The Japanese, too, did not sit idly by. Wakizaka, Kuki and their lieutenants gathered to concoct a sortie. Wakizaka kept his expectations realistic – the goal of the sortie was not to inflict some decisive defeat, but to harass the Joseon fleet and contribute to their exhaustion. The plan was to send a small squadron of sekibune out and then retreat to lure Joseon ships into firing range of the batteries in the forts. For Wakizaka, giving his troops an opportunity to take some offensive action and retaliate would surely raise their morale. A young samurai, possibly named Kunawa Chikakatsu, volunteered enthusiastically to lead the sortie.

On 18d 2m, the sortie squadron sailed out of Ungpo. To their surprise, the Joseon fleet fell back, seemingly in a feigned retreat. But confident in their speed, the Japanese pressed forward. Suddenly, a force of geobukseon and panokseon emerged from their right flank. The darkness and morning mist had hidden this force from view and now they emerged in a counterattack. The Japanese ships immediately retreated, seeing that the bait was taken, albeit not in the way they expected. Eight sekibune managed to get clear, but a panokseon captained by Left Forward Commander Yi Sol and left Geobukseon Captain Lee Eon-ryang's *Bangdapgwiseon* managed to catch up to three Japanese boats. The Joseon crews showered them with arrows, inflicting heavy casualties. The young Japanese commander, clad in scarlet armour and a gold helmet, was directing his men to row quickly when he was shot dead by an arrow. His death, though, seemingly had the effect of inspiring his men to row harder, and the boat managed to slip back to safety in the depths of the bay. One witness later recounted, 'the Japanese mourned loudly over the body of their commander killed in action'. Seeing the cost of the sortie, Wakizaka hunkered his forces down and passed the initiative back to Yi. It was imperative that Yi capture Ungpo before attacking Busan, in order to safeguard his lines of communication. Yi came to the conclusion that victory at Ungpo could only be achieved via land forces – if the Japanese refused to fight on sea, then Yi would take the fight to them on land. The situation was different than in the spring of 1592: victories at Jinju and Pyongyang, as well as countless guerrilla successes, had shown that the Japanese could be beaten on both land and sea. Yi sent a letter to Gyeongsang commissioner Kim Song-il requesting him to join the attack on Ungpo, and, anticipating that the Japanese would evacuate Busan before a major Ming–Joseon land

Kwak Jae-u, a civilian nobleman who raised and equipped his own volunteer army, was the most famous of the Joseon Righteous Army guerrilla commanders. Known for his distinctive red clothing, he played a key role at the first siege of Jinju in distracting the Japanese siege force. His favourite tactic was to use musicians to conceal the size of his small force. (From the War Memorial of Korea)

offensive, deployed his own ships between Chilcheollyang in Geoje Island and Gadeok. This position cut off the force at Ungpo from Busan. Kim had no troops and was busy working to arrange for the arrival of the Ming army, so he instead dispatched a guerrilla force led by Kwak Jae-u, but as of the first month of 1593, Kwak had only 2,000 men in his Righteous Army – too few to be effective against the many thousands of Japanese stationed at Ungpo.

On the 20th, the Joseon fleet engaged the Japanese, but the strong wind and waves tossed the panokseon about. Seeing his crews struggling to control their own ships, Yi blew a horn and signalled with a flag to cancel the attack. Disaster was averted as four ships had collided, but without serious damage. Impatient with the lack of decisive action, Yi decided to risk a raid into the depths of Ungpo bay without waiting for Kwak, who was operating against the Japanese at Changwon. On the 22nd, Yi and his officers held a council of war, concluding that they needed to take it upon themselves to provide the land attack they sought. Though Yi had few troops, the advantage of using his own marines was the unified chain of command that would not have been the case if Yi was attempting to coordinate with a land army. Additionally, the terrain severely limited the number of ships Yi could send in, but he was banking on the hope that the skirmishes in the past several days had weakened the Japanese force enough for an attack by a reduced Joseon force to have a chance at success. Indeed, one rescued Korean prisoner recounted seeing inside Ungcheon: 'We saw many of their war dead cremated by turns… From the end of First Moon [January] infectious diseases spread in the enemy's lines, taking many lives.'

Yi dispatched a provisional squadron of 15 ships, five from each regional fleet, into Ungpo bay. At the same time, he packed 1,700 monk soldiers and marines into ten ships and directed them in a pincer manoeuvre to seize the mountain fortifications – 1,100 landed at Jepo and occupied the old castle there, while 600 landed further east behind the Baekseoksan mountain and made camp. Startled by the sudden appearance of Joseon troops on their flanks, the Japanese responded immediately, attacking the Joseon beachheads, but the Joseon troops fought hard, with the monk

Recognizing the need for a popular resistance at all levels of society against the Japanese, King Seonjo met with the Buddhist monk leader Hyujeong in 5m 1592, and asked him to issue a call to arms to resist the Japanese invasion, to which thousands answered. In late summer of 1592, some 400 monks joined Yi's navy, and, finding them to be capable and resolute men, Yi promoted many on the spot to be officers in his assault units. Two monks, Samhye and Uinung, were each made captain of their own panokseon and operated as a detached force with mixed guerrilla and garrison duties. This particular painting shows Hyujeong leading his volunteers to attack the Japanese garrison at Pyongyang. (From the War Memorial of Korea)

EVENTS

1. 1,100 marines and monk soldiers disembark at Jepo Castle and another 600 land north of Baekseoksan mountain.
2. Japanese troops attack Jepo Castle, but are repulsed.
3. Fifteen panokseon enter Ungpo bay and bombard the Japanese fleet.
4. As they withdraw, they come under fire from the mountain forts and two panokseon collide. They are grappled and boarded by Japanese troops, who pursue the Joseon ships out of the bay.
5. The Jindo panokseon is also attacked as it exits the bay. Due to Won Gyun's inaction, Lee Mong-gu's squadron intervenes to rescue it.

Fragmented pieces of a daejanggunjeon, the largest of the Joseon anti-ship arrows and fired from the Cheonja chongtong. (From the collection of the National Museum of Korea, accessible at https://www.emuseum.go.kr/)

soldiers launching counterattacks at every point, ably supported by the sharp fire of the marines. The ground combat lasted all day long, and the Japanese withdrew after suffering heavy losses, though in good order, as they seemed to have recovered the bodies of their dead such that the Joseon troops did not collect many heads. The naval assault also went well, sinking dozens of ships in their moorings before withdrawing.

However, growing overconfident with their victory, two captains, Lee Ung-gae of the Jeolla Left Navy and Lee Kyong-jip of the Jeolla Right Navy, began to compete over who could sink the most ships. They led two of their ships each into Ungpo without orders, but in their recklessness, the Balpo panokseon and the Garipo panokseon collided and ran aground as they were sailing back out, destroying the shielding on their upper decks. This golden opportunity was not lost on Wakizaka, who ordered a general counterattack and ran to his sekibune, as did Kuki. Wakizaka had prepared for this moment. Because the panokseon were so large and could not easily be boarded, Wakizaka had equipped his ships with ropes and harpoons to aid in capturing Joseon ships. The mountain fort garrison poured fire into the hapless Joseon squadron, and some Japanese even managed to board the ships. In a mass panic to avoid the barrage of arrows and shot, the now-exposed sailors all rushed to the other side of the ship and tipped over the sturdy panokseon. Of those who swam to shore, several deserted back home. Choi Man-chun, a Joseon officer of the Gyeongsang Right Navy who had been held prisoner in Ungcheon, recounted after his rescue:

> On the 22nd of Second Moon, when our navy came to attack the enemy by landing and by attacking the enemy vessels at their moorings, the Japanese in the town, being all aged and sick, hurried to and fro at a loss of what to do, and twelve Japanese chiefs were even going to kill themselves by jumping into the sea. Just then, two of our board-roofed ships collided and capsized on the narrow river. Seeing this, a Japanese vice-commander [Kumagai Inosuke, one of Wakizaka's men] jumped on the sinking ship only to be pierced in the chest by a long spear thrown by a Korean sailor. Death was instantaneous.

Urging his crews to row at speed, Kuki managed to grab hold of a panokseon via a grappling hook (Japanese accounts have this incident occurring on 21d 2m). As he was reeling up to the Joseon ship, Wakizaka pulled alongside, spear in hand. The spirit of competition seems to have infected the Japanese camp as well, and Wakizaka, proclaiming that the prize was his, ordered his men to cut the grappling hook! Two of his retainers, Mibusuke and Sokuji, slashed the rope, but the panokseon bounded forwards to safety, denying both samurai their glory. The Jindo panokseon (one of Yi Eok-gi's ships) was also swarmed as it exited Ungpo. Much to Yi's infuriation, Won Gyun ignored the plight of the Jindo ship, so a squadron of geobukseon and panokseon under Lee Mong-gu rushed to save it, forming a hagik-jin and blasting away the Japanese ships surrounding the panokseon. Japanese naval records have it that Kato was able to capture a panokseon, but it is uncertain if this is one of the panokseon that capsized, the Jindo ship that was almost taken or another ship entirely.

The action on the 22nd was without result, with both sides suffering heavy casualties, and the narrow escapes as well as the loss of two panokseon warned Yi to the difficulties of attacking Ungpo. Yi blamed himself for failing to exert greater control over his captains and wrote to the court that he would take full responsibility for the loss of the two panokseon. Yi says nothing more on his landing force, which was likely re-embarked after finding the Japanese positions on the mountains and at Ungcheon too strong to attack by itself, or perhaps found its position untenable. If Yi was to safely attack the Japanese fleet, then he needed to destroy the coastal defences first. On the 28th, Yi launched another, more ferocious, naval bombardment on the mountain forts, laying down an intense fire and shooting bigyeokjincheonroe. But without ground troops, the Joseon navy could not capture the mountains by itself and fell back having failed to eliminate the coastal fortifications.

Various Joseon weapons: a janggunjeon loaded into a cannon, a bigyeokjincheonroe and a wangu mortar. (Photograph by Yuhan Kim, from the Korea National Science Museum)

The blockade of Ungpo carried into the third month. Yi was frustrated at the lack of news from high command regarding the grand offensive to drive the Japanese expeditionary force out, only knowing that the Ming army under Li Rusong had been defeated at the battle of Byeokjegwan on 26d 1m, and that it had retreated back north. Kwon Jun fell ill, seriously enough that Yi saw him off from the front. Another desultory firefight with the land batteries occurred on 6d 3m. On the 10th, the wind was blowing northwards, so Yi outfitted several fire ships to send into the moored fleet, but cancelled the attack. The reason he gave the royal court was his repeated concern that if the Ming army was not there to seal Ungpo off from land, the Japanese would move deeper inland and kill civilians as they went. By the latter half of the third month, the Joseon navy was exhausted and running low on supplies. They had been on campaign for two months, and the ship crews were needed at home to plough the fields and prepare for the autumn harvest. Also, by this point, the diseases ravaging the Japanese camp were beginning to creep into the Joseon fleet. So on 3d 4m, Yi ended the blockade of Ungpo and ordered his fleet to disperse, with the men returning to their farms and the ships going into harbour for long-overdue repairs.

The results of the battle of Ungpo are debated. Some Korean historians see it as a victory, though the Joseon court did not see the operation as a success at the time, clearly referring to it as a failure. Tactically, the Koreans had ravaged the Ungpo fleet, sinking 50 ships and causing hundreds of casualties with their incessant attacks. Many more Japanese had died from disease caused by the conditions of the blockade. The Japanese could claim victory in denying the enemy a victory as they had prevented an annihilation of their fleet, and even managed to sink two panokseon – but at the cost of many of their own ships. Their Fabian strategy had prevented Yi from doing as much damage as he had hoped, and in the months-long campaign, the Joseon navy had expended the stockpiles of food and munitions that

Yi had carefully amassed. Indeed, Yi's fleet would suffer from the logistical expense of this costly operation for the rest of 1593. Korean casualties are unknown, but were likely heavier than any previous engagement given the protracted nature of the campaign. Strategically, the Japanese could claim victory on the grounds that by preventing the Koreans from destroying the Ungpo base, they had kept Yi from achieving his objective of attacking Busan and saved the fleet there. The Koreans could claim some strategic success in that they had tied up thousands of Japanese troops who could have been deployed elsewhere on the peninsula. Yi's attack on Ungpo was one of many relentless assaults on Hideyoshi's expeditionary force in early 1593, and, coupled with the advance of the Ming and remnants of the Joseon Royal Army in the North, Kwon Yul's army, the Jeolla garrisons and hundreds of guerrilla bands, it led to the Japanese retreat to the coast later that year. In any case, however, it is clear that the Joseon fleet fell short of its desired objectives and the Japanese had successfully defended Busan.

Yi cannot be faulted for the failure to find a decisive victory at Ungpo. He had gone to Ungpo on the promise of a coordinated land attack, which he knew was the only way to achieve victory. The Joseon court also absolved Yi of blame, acknowledging that any effort against Ungpo and Ungcheon would have to be spearheaded by the army, not the navy. Much to his credit, Yi kept up the blockade for two whole months, waiting in vain for support, and even stretching his limited resources to launch his own land attack. For the Koreans, the failure was at a strategic level and the misinterpretation of Japanese intentions in the wake of the fall of Pyongyang. Yes, the Japanese invasion force was rattled at the start of 1593, but it would take a worsening strategic situation before they abandoned Hanyang at last. And even when they did, Hideyoshi had no intention of abandoning his campaign so easily. In the fourth month of 1593, the Joseon court discussed:

> Who wouldn't be concerned about the Japanese sending more troops this spring? According to Ryu Seong-ryong's report from last time, 'Yi Sun-sin captured a Japanese ship transporting food, and Park Ui-jang captured a Japanese pirate who was making new clothes.' So there is no doubt that they are sending more troops. And there is talk that countless Japanese ships have arrived and are anchoring, so tell the Office of Military Affairs to devise further measures.

The Ungpo campaign also showed growing signs of tensions in the Joseon camp. In the combined fleet, Yi was growing frustrated with Won Gyun's unprofessionalism. Yi disapproved of the careless way Won led his troops and wrote reports with exaggerations. He also disliked Won's crude behaviour, including his excessive drinking, and thought his tactical acumen to be lacking. Won on the other hand disliked working under Yi, jealous of his successes. Then there was the problem of the information gap between the central court and the naval commanders. The intricacies of the tactical situation along the southern coast of Korea, things that were only known to the local commanders, were lost to the Joseon high command. This would not be the last time the Joseon court, operating on a poor understanding of the situation on the Korean coast, would order a naval offensive – with disastrous consequences.

AFTERMATH

On 19m 5d 1593, the Japanese army, hungry, exhausted and disease-ridden, retreated from Hanyang. The strategic situation of the war had shifted dramatically since the initial lightning advance up the Korean Peninsula in the summer of 1592. After 11 months of campaigning, Hideyoshi's initial invasion force of 158,800 men had suffered over 60 per cent casualties. Yi's navy had a direct role in liberating Hanyang. In the third month of 1593, Yi dispatched a convoy under Jeong Geol to support the advance of Field Marshal Kwon Yul's army on Hanyang. Jeong played a decisive role in Kwon's victory at the battle of Haengju on 12d 2m, when he arrived with supplies and reinforcements just when the outnumbered Joseon army had exhausted their arrows and munitions. With the Ming army to their front and Kwon Yul on their flank, the Japanese position in Hanyang was no longer tenable.

From 1593 onwards, the Imjin War shifted southwards, with the Japanese hunkering down on the defensive in Gyeongsang to try and maintain a beachhead. For the next four years, both sides would enter an uneasy truce, all the while preparing for the next round of fighting. The Japanese doubled down on their coastal defence strategy, building a network of *wajo* (stone castles) across the Gyeongsang coastline. Some half of the initial expeditionary force remained, while the other half constructed the fortifications at Busan, Ungcheon, Sacheon, Ulsan, Geoje and Dangpo, among many other places. The wajo strategy was likely informed by the effectiveness of coastal fortifications in preventing total defeat at Busan and Ungpo. To address their own supply problems, the Japanese both imported more supplies and began to grow their own. The Korean civilians who lived in this occupied zone had a strange coexistence with the occupying Japanese garrisons. Some carried on with their daily lives, coexisting alongside the Japanese army. An escaped POW named Choi Man-chun reported seeing 'four hundred sailors' families from Chonsong and Gadeok work on the farm and harvest crops as usual, with 20 Japanese as

Reconstructions of three geobukseon and a panokseon at the Donam Tourist Complex in Tongyeong, with accessible interiors. All of the geobukseon appear to follow the two and two-and-a-half level model. (Photograph by Kim Ji-ho, Korea Tourism Organization)

their chiefs'. The Korean captives taken in the war who were kept in the Japanese bases were not so fortunate and were used as forced labour on ships and castles, with some possibly forced into sexual slavery.

The Japanese navy was extremely active during this lull. Larger ships of sturdier construction, purpose-built to combat the Joseon navy, were being built in ports across Japan. Convoys of hundreds of ships packed with sick and wounded from months of campaigning sailed back to Japan, returning loaded with grains that were stored in Busan and distributed to the various Japanese garrisons. The losses of 1592–93 were made up for by the arrival of fresh squadrons. In all some 700–800 ships were deployed at the wajo and other forward bases to screen Busan as Ungpo had done. Moving at night, they leapt from Ungpo out to other bays, quickly gaining ground and establishing a front line around Geoje Island. On 17d 4m, the Joseon court issued an order for Yi to embark on a sixth sortie to destroy the convoys of reinforcements coming from Japan and make another raid on Busan, but this was easier said than done and the concentration of Japanese ships at Geoje made such a raid difficult. Won Gyun wrote to the court in June:

> The Japanese pirates in Ungcheon and Changwon are still entrenched, and the Japanese pirates in Ungpo have gradually increased and are twice as strong as before, but they have occupied the dangerous terrain and are not coming out.

This painting at the Jeseungdang shows life at the Yeosu naval base. In the foreground are several civilians, likely refugees, hired to make and repair weapons. Several Joseon military officers stand behind them, and in the background is the port that houses a portion of the Jeolla Left Navy. (Courtesy of the Jeseungdang)

> The enemies anchored in the two rivers of Gimhae and Yangsan are taking turns entering and leaving, relying on each other like teeth, and controlling the route to Busan… If we leave these enemy dens alone and enter Busan as they are, the enemies in front and behind will attack us from both inside and out, so it is truly dangerous … it would be best to first attack Ungpo and then gradually attack Gimhae and Yangsan, annihilating the enemies here and there and opening the route to Busan.

Two could play the game of jockeying for positions, and Yi built a forward base called Haeyoung on Hansando in the seventh month to block Japanese incursions into his waters. Yi's ships engaged in a standoff against them, with neither side moving to give battle – the Japanese would not meet the Joseon fleet in open water, while the latter would not advance into the maze-like coastline. Japanese ships ventured into Yi's waters, but fled at first sight of the pursuit squadrons Yi dispatched. Meanwhile on land, in June the Japanese launched a punitive expedition against Jinju with a large army, managing to breach the fortress and massacring the entire populace after a second siege. The Joseon court attempted to take advantage of this offensive by planning an attack of their own into the lightly held Japanese bases. But with their army in disarray and the next wave of Ming reinforcements still forthcoming, no such attack materialized.

Yi, too, was busy preparing for a renewed offensive. Impressed with the penetration power of Japanese firearms, Yi put together a team of officers and smiths to successfully reverse-engineer the Japanese arquebus and streamlined its production process such that every port and town under Yi's jurisdiction was mass-producing them. The fleet was being expanded as well, with Yi ordering Yi Eok-gi to build 19 more panokseon and Won Gyun to build 40 panokseon and 40 hyeopseon by the new year. In all, Yi planned to build 150 panokseon and 150 hyeopseon in total for the combined Jeolla navies.

While Yi had no trouble building ships, the problem was procuring manpower and ordinance – a fleet of that size needed 29,000 men. Yi was fighting an uphill logistical battle. The messengers he sent to search for artillery pieces scattered at various army depots and a call for spare iron yielded little fruit, so he suggested that the court offer military exemptions or emancipation from slavery for those who donated iron to the navy. Between the privations of war and the pillaging of the Ming army, Jeolla Province was starved of food. Additionally, the Jeolla Left Navy was facing a critical manpower shortage. Of the 6,200 men under Yi's command at the start of the Ungpo campaign, some 600 alone had died of disease by the eighth month. Many more deserted, causing Yi to lament the numerous vacancies in his fleet and that 'half the numbers of the so-called adults who have been enlisted from the coastal areas of the three naval stations, though registered, are riff-raff, with only a few competent fighters'. Even Hong Tae-su, an officer on the *Suncheongwiseon* geobukseon of the formidable Suncheon squadron, was executed for desertion. Weighing the hardship that substitute drafts would impose on civilians but desperate for troops, Yi reluctantly asked the court for authorization to substitute drafts, but this was countermanded by a decree from Crown Prince Gwanghae (for the former reason).

Yi also found himself in constant competition with the army, which was conscripting from naval districts in spite of repeated requests to stop. Land-based monk guerrilla leaders also came into Yi's naval districts to recruit away

A painting of Yi training his marines. The troops wear the black-and-white *pojol-bok*, the Joseon constabulary dress, which is popularly represented in media as the standard Joseon military uniform. In combat, the Yi's marines would have worn light armor or helmets over the pojol-bok. In the background, Joseon light cavalry armed with lances practise a charge. While a naval commander, Yi still devoted considerable concern to the army. He most certainly had a contingent of cavalry that was used to guard the base or support nearby garrison posts. (From the Korean Naval Academy Museum)

Yi's own monk sailor-marines while they were resting at their temples. Not even Yi's officers were immune from the inter-branch competition over manpower – Song Yo-chong, who had been dispatched north to procure supplies, had never returned, having been snatched up by another unit and reassigned. Yi pleaded with the court 'not to transfer magistrates in naval service or border commanders of sea defence to other places but to attach them solely to the navy'.

In his diary entry for 1d 7m 1593, Yi writes that he was unable to sleep and sat alone by a bonfire, lost in thoughts and in a state of unease about the war. This entry captures the essence of the endless days and sleepless nights Yi spent racking his brain, alone and often ill from exhaustion and stress, to find ways to address his logistical problems. He devised a plan to resettle refugees and his wounded on abandoned horse farms that were fertile and create state-owned farms to draw provisions from, but the Joseon court was wary, questioning if there was sufficient manpower to enact Yi's plan. Yi also asked for permission to hold his own military service examinations in order to give his men a formal opportunity to be promoted, which they had been thus far denied due to the chaos of the war. The pressure mounted on Yi in the final months of 1593. His relationship with Won Gyun worsened, and Yi bemoaned Won's lack of discipline and deceitful behavior, causing Yi to worry, 'If we continue to work together in this manner, will there not be problems later on?' Complaining that 'However, since reporting that they [Joseon navy] won the battle [of Busan] last year, they have not defeated the enemy even once', some in the Joseon high command sought to investigate and punish the naval commanders for failing to provide victories. When one official questioned, 'Is Yi Sun-sin perhaps being lazy?' Ryu Seong-ryong retorted, 'If it weren't for Yi Sun-sin, it would have been difficult to get this far. Yi Sun-sin is the best of all of our generals on land and sea.' Even King Seonjo weighed in, saying that the Joseon military was in no state to go on the offensive.

Indeed, the Joseon military was in a state of logistical disarray. Any future offensive would have to be launched in tandem with more Ming troops, as those in Korea were deemed too few, but reinforcements were still forthcoming. The Joseon court was consumed in debate on how to break the stalemate, and were rightly concerned that the Japanese were building up a force within their strongholds to launch a counterattack in the spring of 1594. To prevent this, they suggested in September that the navy, with support from the cavalry, engage in constant raids to wear down the Japanese. In November, the Joseon court weighed a simultaneous offensive in tandem with the Ming expeditionary force, but decided against it for a lack of troops and siege engines.

Without men, and with the Japanese dug in, there was little Yi could do to change the situation at sea. In these lonely and rainy times, Yi writes that he found comfort when his children visited him and he heard news that his mother was in good health. On one particular day (12d 8m 1593), when Yi 'was so sick that I lay down all day and groaned. I forced myself to sit up even though my clothes were soaked with cold sweat', Yi Sun-sin (M) and Kwon Jun came by and kept Yi company all day, playing Jjangi while he watched.

The Joseon court recognized Yi's achievements and talents by promoting him in the eighth month of 1593 to a new position made just for him – *Samdosugun Tongjesa* (Naval Commander of the Three Provinces), giving Yi chief command over the Gyeongsang, Jeolla and Chungcheong navies. Yi had partly assumed the de facto role of this position before its creation out of necessity, but as Samdosugun Tongjesa, he had official authority and could now better coordinate three provincial navies. The self-effacing Yi responded to his promotion with characteristic humility: 'At this juncture, all unexpectedly, I am being ordered by Your Majesty to assume the office of Supreme Commander of Naval Forces of the Three Provinces, I am awestruck with surprise like one who falls into a deep valley. A mediocre person unequal to the great task, I am the more perplexed with fear.' Thinking of the immense logistical burdens he was managing and concerned over the illness of many of his sailors, Yi gave himself little celebration that day. In truth, there was no one more qualified to command the united fleet.

ANALYSIS AND IMPACT

Yi's naval campaigns were one of several factors that all together forced the retreat of the Japanese army from Hanyang and placed it on a defensive posture for most of the war. At a grand strategic level, the war at sea was a secondary concern to the war on land for the Joseon court, but the one where they found the most success. By defeating the Japanese navy at sea and forcing it to become a 'fleet in being', Yi played a key role in denying Hideyoshi's conquest of Jeolla Province and the turning of the war against the Japanese in 1593. Most importantly, he prevented the Japanese navy from breaking through to the western coast of Korea. Had the Japanese been able to do so, they could have accessed Korea's major rivers and supply troops even deep inland, mitigating the effect of the guerrillas. Additionally, by achieving regional naval supremacy, Yi ensured that Jeolla Province would be a safe base for the Joseon army to operate out of against the Japanese overland supply line. For the people of Joseon, this meant they were protected from the acts of violence that would have come with raids against an undefended coast.

Yi's greatest contribution to the Joseon war effort in 1592–93 related to morale. He gave Joseon Korea its first victory in the war at Okpo, and the string of victories that followed restored the broken confidence of the Joseon military.

Shocked by the defeats, the Japanese daimyos avoided battle, giving Yi mastery of the seas, but not the coastal inlets. They quickly adapted to Joseon naval tactics. If offensive victory could not be had, then they worked to deny the Joseon fleet its objectives by maximizing the use of terrain to safeguard their fleets. The ad hoc Japanese response ultimately denied Yi the decisive victory he sought after Hansando, as the Japanese were able to maintain their lines of communication to Japan. As the Ungpo operation showed, a protracted operation to blockade Busan would have been impossible unless the ground troops were working in tandem. The Japanese recovered quickly from the material losses suffered in 1592 – by 1593, their fleet was larger than before. With the Joseon fleet crippled in the second half of 1593 due to manpower shortages and unable to afford a costly attack against well-defended Japanese ports, the Japanese were able to expand their naval reaches, albeit with caution.

Victory for Yi, however, was by no means assured simply by the asymmetry in technology and tactics – the opponents Yi faced were no amateurs. Unfamiliar with his foes and having never fought a naval battle, Yi approached his initial campaigns with prudent caution. His conduct of war and victories were textbook-like, coming from an early recognition of the strengths and weaknesses of the Joseon and Japanese navies. He encouraged ranged combat in his directions to his captains while eschewing melee unless it was absolutely necessary or victory was guaranteed. A large part of Yi's tactical success stemmed from the tight control he held over his fleet – no easy task in an age where captains sought personal glory and ships were crewed by less-than-willing conscripts. He drilled his men constantly and conducted exercises whenever he had the chance, preparations that showed their value in the excellent combat performance of the Joseon fleet. Effective communication with his captains set the groundwork for the precise formation deployments and coordinated attacks seen in his battles. His disciplinarian methods ensured that his navy functioned and critical tasks were carried out in what was otherwise an inefficient and often corrupt military.

Yi pursued the decisive victory of annihilation, the same ruthless streak possessed by other great captains. He masterfully employed terrain, hiding his squadrons in the undulating coastline to outflank his foes. After each battle, he contemplated how a more complete victory could have been achieved if there were effective land forces to coordinate with. Yi was highly cognizant of the interdependence between land and sea forces, and displayed a refreshing lack of selfishness when it came to cooperating with Joseon's ground troops. In 1592, when there were enough supplies to go around, he often used naval stores to supply the fortresses and garrison posts of Jeolla Province. Rather than keep all of the conscripts and recruits his officers gathered for the navy, Yi distributed them as needed to land forces as well. It was a gesture that paid dividends by ensuring the security of the province, and with it, the Yeosu naval base. Yi's 1592 campaigns won him renown, but the Imjin War still had five more devastating years to play out, and Yi's finest hour that would enshrine him as Korea's greatest military hero was yet to come.

THE BATTLEFIELDS TODAY

The Imjin War and the campaigns of Admiral Yi have been the subject of numerous media depictions, notably the 2004 KBS TV drama *Immortal Admiral Yi Sun-sin*. Most recently is a successful trilogy of movies about Admiral Yi's battles directed by Kim Han-min: *The Admiral: Roaring Currents* (2014), *Hansan: Rising Dragon* (2022) and *Noryang: Deadly Sea* (2023). South Korea abounds with museums that relate to the campaigns in this book. The first is the National War Memorial and Museum in Seoul. The museum covers Korean military history as a whole, and includes an excellent exhibition on the Imjin War and a large model of a geobukseon. The basement complex underneath Gwanghwamun Plaza also houses a large exhibition about Admiral Yi. No visit to South Korea is complete without a trip to Jinju, the site of two key Imjin War battles. The inner keep of the former fortress has been reconstructed to house a large park with several memorials to the battles. At the centre of the park is the Jinju National Museum, the place to go for all things related to Joseon military history. The Jinju National Museum also runs an excellent YouTube channel covering the technology and logistics of the Joseon military, with

Jinju fortress, as viewed from the river side. The museum is out of the frame but located further left. A path from the Chokseongnu pavilion leads to the water's edge and a memorial to Nongae. After the second siege of Jinju where the Japanese took the fortress and were slaughtering all the garrison and inhabitants, a group of samurai were celebrating their victory at the pavilion. A woman named Nongae lured one of the samurai to the water's edge, grabbed him and jumped, drowning them both. (Photograph by Kim Ji-ho, Korea Tourism Organization)

many of their videos subtitled in English. At Yi's hometown of Asan, there is a dedicated Yi Sun-sin Museum complex.

The commemoration and preservation of the Imjin War battlefields varies greatly from location to location. At Yeosu, one can still trace remnants of the Jeolla Left Navy's headquarters. The primary remaining structure is the Jinnamgwan, a large building that served as a guest house at the base and has been preserved, repaired and rebuilt to this day.

Okpo is now a major shipyard, but visitors seeking to retrace the 1592 campaign will not be disappointed. A large memorial park commemorates Korea's first victory in the Imjin War. The park has a well-maintained museum with Joseon-era artefacts, weaponry, model ships and dioramas of the battle. Sights related to the battle of Hansando are concentrated in the city of Tongyeong. There is a reconstructed geobukseon, and every summer the city holds a festival to commemorate the battle. While not directly related to Yi's campaigns, the Samdosugun Tongjeyeong, created in 1604 as the headquarters of the Samdosugun Tongjesa, is also located in Tongyeong. While only the Seobbyeongwan guesthouse survived the destruction of government buildings in the Japanese colonial occupation, the rest of the compound has been reconstructed to its former glory as when Yi's successors worked there.

The coastline of Busan looks nothing like it did in 1592, and the original battlefield where the Japanese ships would have been anchored has largely been built over.

Hansando is accessible by a regularly scheduled ferry. The island houses the reconstructed Jeseungdang at the site of the Jeolla Left Navy's former base on the island. The well-maintained complex houses several buildings

The Jinnamgwan at Yeosu. It was first constructed in 1599 and rebuilt in 1718 after a fire. (Photograph by Kim Ji-ho, Korea Tourism Organization)

The Yi Sun-sin memorial park in Tongyeong, South Korea. The large seaside park and walking course are among the city's most popular attractions. (Photograph by Song Jae-geun, Korea Tourism Organization)

of interest, namely the Jeseungdang, which served as Yi's office and is today decorated with paintings of his victories and displays of his decorations. There is also the Chungmusa shrine, which is dedicated to Yi and houses a portrait of him.

The remnants of the Japanese wajo castles are perhaps the most significant physical traces left of the Imjin War. The sturdy stone foundations, the last vestiges of an invasion, are all that remain, and their states vary from ruins to integration into urban settings. The Ungcheon wajo is little more than its crumbling foundations, overgrown with vegetation, and many others are similarly forgotten piles of rocks. The Busanjin fortress, the Japanese fortress built over the original Joseon one, remained active under the Joseon dynasty after the war. What remains are reconstructions of the Joseon-style gates. The stone foundations of the nearby Japanese fortress on Jeungsan today serve as a park for the local community.

Hansando Island today. A geobukseon-shaped lighthouse and a mountaintop monument (which can be seen in the background) commemorate the battle. (Photograph by Song Jae-geun, Korea Tourism Organization)

The Jeseungdang on Hansando Island, where Yi established a forward base. Today it houses a shrine, display, walking trail and several structures of interest related to Yi's time on the island. (Photograph by Song Jae-geun, Korea Tourism Organization)

BIBLIOGRAPHY

BOOKS

Do Hyun-shin, *Yi Sun-sin and the Joseon-Japan War* (행복한미래, 2012)
Hawley, Samuel, *The Imjin War: Japan's 16th-century Invasion of Korea and Attempt to Conquer China* (Conquistador Press, 2014)
Hwang Hyun-Pil, *Yi Sun-sin's Sea* (역바연, 2021)
Jinju National Museum, *The Age of Gunpowder in Joseon* (Jinju National Museum, 2021)
Jung Gwang-su, *Yi Sun-sin and the Imjin War*, Vols 2 & 3 (비봉출판사, 2005)
Kim So-young (ed.), *Memory and Evaluation of Muui-gong Yi Sun-sin in the Imjin War* (Gwangmyeong Cultural Center, 2020)
Kitajima Manji, *Toyotomi Hideyoshi Chōsen shinryaku kankei shiryō shūsei* 北島万次『豊臣秀吉朝鮮侵略関係史料集成』Vols 1 & 2 (Heibonsha, 2017)
Swope, Kenneth, *A Dragon's Head and a Serpent's Tail* (University of Oklahoma Press, 2009)
Toyotomi Hideyoshi, *Monjoshū* 豊臣秀吉文書集, Vol. 5 (Yoshikawa Kōbunkan, 2015–17)
Turnbull, Stephen, *Samurai Invasion: Japan's Korean War 1592–1598* (Cassell, 2002)
Yi Sun-sin, Choi Doo-hyun (trans.) 난중일기 [*Nanjung Ilgi*] (학민사, 1996)
Yi Sun-sin, Ha Tae-hung (trans.) *Imjin Chang'cho: Admiral Yi Sun-sin's Memorials to Court* (Annyeong Books, 2014)
Yi Sun-sin, Ha Tae-hung (trans.), Sohn Pow-key (ed.), *Nanjung ilgi: War Diary of Admiral Yi Sun-sin* (Yonsei University Press, 1977)

ARTICLES

Cha Cheol-uk, 'Examination of Materials Related Japanese Navy's Activity in Japanese Invasion of Korea in 1592', *Busan National University Journal of Koreanology*, 27, pp.95–128 (2006)
Hong Soon-gu, 'A Study on the Structure of the Panok warship and Yi sun-sin's Byeolje Turtle Ship in the Imjin War', 조형미디어학, 22.2, pp.188–99 (2019)
Hur Nam-lin, 'The Japanese Invasion of Korea in 1592: Current Research Trends among Korean, Japanese, and English-speaking Scholars', *International Journal of Korean History*, 18(2), pp.53–80 (2013)
Hur Nam-lin, 'National Defense in Shambles: Wartime Military Buildup in Chosŏn Korea, 1592–98', *Seoul Journal of Korean Studies*, 22(2), pp.113–35 (2009)
Jae Jang-myung, 'The Role of Subordinates of Yi Sun-sin During the Japanese Invasion of 1592–1598', *History and Borders*, 52, pp.1–45 (2004)
Jae Jang-myung, 'The Status and Activities of Gyeongsang Left Navy during the Imjin War', Institute for Military History, 109, pp.281–320 (2018)
Kim Byung-ryun, 'Study on Panokseon Crews', 이순신연구논총, 20, pp.169–217 (2013)
Park Joo-mi, 'A Study on Japanese Naval Forces Participating in the Japanese Invasion of Korea in Imjin', *Journal of Korean Maritime Security*, 6(2), pp.109–34 (2023)
Roh Young-koo, 'Yi Sun-shin, an Admiral Who Became a Myth', *The Review of Korean Studies*, 7(3), pp.15–36 (2004)
Shin Yoon-ho, 'Comparison of the Korean and Japanese Naval Forces in the Early Naval Battles of the Imjin War', *Military and Culture Association of Korea-Japan*, 37, pp.120–47 (2023)

WEBSITES

森甚一郎, '阿波水軍と朝鮮の役', 郷土研究発表会第9号 https://library.bunmori.tokushima.jp/digital/webkiyou/09/0906.htm

Virtual Touken Museum, Token Corporation, www.touken-world.jp/

Jae Jang-myung, 'Battle of Hansando and Joseon Navy Tactics', Korea Maritime Security Forum (2018), http://komsf.or.kr/bbs/board.php?bo_table=m45&wr_id=56

Lee Ki-hwan, 'The brutal Battle of Dongnae Castle that made even the excavators cry... What happened on April 15, 1592?', Gyeongsang News (May 2021), www.khan.co.kr/article/202105170600001

National Institute of Korean History, https://history.go.kr/

戦国時代勢力図と各大名の動向 https://sengokumap.net/

디지털창원문화대전, https://changwon.grandculture.net/changwon

http://myarmoury.com/feature_jpn_armour.php

INDEX

Figures in **bold** refer to illustrations.

Angolpo 11, **44**, 53, 59, **61**
archery 10, **17**, 29–30, **31**, 33, 35, **46**, 59
armour 4, **18**, 21, **22**, **27**, **28**, 30, **33**, **34**, 35, 43, 45, 52, **54**, 58, **60**, **64**, **75**, 76
arquebusiers 4, 33, 35, **64**
artillery **24**, **25**, 28, 30, 36, 59, **64**, **72**, 85
Asan 12, **14**, 90
ashigaru (Japanese feudal infantry) 4, **22**–23, 33, **59**, **60**, **64**
atakebune (Japanese warship) 21, **34**, 35, 42, 45–47, 50, 51, 55, 57–58, **59**, **64**, **65**, 67, 68–69

Bae Hong-rip 17, 45
Balpo 11–12, 17, 80
Bangdap 11, 17–18, 29, 52
barracks **72**, 73
batteries 28, 59–60, **72**, 73, 76, 81
battles:
 battle of Anegawa 22
 battle of Angolpo 9, 21, 30, 58, **61**, **64**, 66
 battle of Busan 4, 6, 7, 8–9, **18**, 19, 28, 66, **72**, 74, 83, 86
 battle of Byeokjegwan 9, 81
 battle of Chilcheollyang 13, 16
 battle of Chungju 7, 8, 38, **66**
 battle of Danghangpo 8, 43, **44**, **51**, 53
 battle of Dangpo 8, 43, **44**, 47, 50
 battle of Dongnae 6, 8
 first battle of Geumsan Mountain 9
 second battle of Geumsan Mountain 9
 battle of Haengju 9, 83
 battle of Hansando 8, 20, 53, **56**, **57**, 58, 59, **64**, 66, 68, 88, 90
 battle of Happo 8, **39**
 battle of Ichi 8, **66**
 battle of the Imjin River 7, 8
 battle of Janglimpo 9, **68**
 battle of Jeokjinpo 8, **39**, 42
 battle of Kizugawaguchi 21
 second battle of Kizugawaguchi 21, **35**
 battle of Mikijozeme 19
 battle of Noryang **14**, 21, 38, 45
 battle of Okpo 8, **15**, **29**, **31**, 37, **39**, **41**, 42, **52**, 53, 55, 58, 88
 fourth battle of Pyongyang 9, 74–76
 battle of Sacheon 8, 43, **44**, 45, 46
 battle of Sekigahara 21, **22**, 23
 battle of Shizugatake 19, 22
 battle of Sojukdo Island 25
 battle of Ungchi 8, 66
 battle of Ungpo 79, 81

 battle of Yongin 8, 55, 74
 battle of Yulpo 8, **44**
bigyeokjincheonroe (Joseon timed-fuse bomb) 26, 55, 57, **81**
Busan 4, 5, 6, 7, 8, 34, 37, 39, 43, **44**, 53–54, 59–61, **67**, **68**, 69, 73–77, 82–85, 88, 90

cannons 21, **24**, **25**, **27**, 29, 30, **31**, 35, **36**, 50, **54**, 55, 57, **64**, 67, 69, **81**
 cannon balls 41, 45, 73, 76
 cannon fire 45, 57, 60–61
 chongtong (Joseon cannons) 24, **25**, **27**, 30, 42, 54, 73, 80
castles:
 Busanjin 68
 Dangpo 47
 Dongnae 5, 6, 8
 Imabari 23
 Jepo 77, 78, 79
 Jeungsan 68
 Joseon 75
 Matsuyama 22
 Nagoya 65
 Shichi 22
 Toba 21
 Ungcheon 75, 78, 79
 wajo (Japanese stone castles) 83, 91
Chugoku 32, 69
Chungmusa shrine **18**, **38**, 91

daejanggunjeon (Joseon arrow missiles) 25, **50**, 60, 64, 80
daimyo (Japanese feudal lord) 5, 22, 23, 32, 34, 46, 69, 88
Danghangpo **44**, 47, **51**, 52
Dangpo 11, 38, **39**, 40, **44**, 46–47, 67, 83
desertion 6, 28, 32, 33, 38, 74, 85
dujeonggap (Joseon brigandine-style armour) **28**, 75

entrenchments 73, 76
Eo Yeong-dam 17–18, 45, 54–55, **56**, 57

fire-arrows 41, 58, 60
flechettes **27**, 45, **54**
fortifications 12, 45, 69, **72**, 73, 75, 77, **79**, 81, 83

Gadeok Island 11, 43, **44**, 53, 59, **61**, 67–68, 73, 76–77, 83
Garipo 11, 80
garrison posts 38, 74, **86**, 88
geobukseon (Joseon turtle ship) **15**, 19, 25, 29, **30**, **31**, 32, 45, 47, **50**, 51, 52, 54–55, **56**, 59, 60, 67, 69, 76, 80, **83**, 85, 89–90, **92**

Geoje Island 7, 12, **39**, 40, 42, **43**, **44**, 47, 53–54, 66, 74, 77, 83–84
Gimhae **44**, 53, 58, 67, 85
Goseong 12, 14, 40
gunpowder **25**, **27**, 29, 36, 58, 73
Gyeongnaeryang 54–55, **56**, 59, 75
Gyeongsang Left Navy 5, 11–12, 34, 38, 41, 46, 67, 87
Gyeongsang Province 4, 7, 11, 24, 38, 66–67, 76, 83
Gyeongsang Right Navy 11–12, 16, 34, 38, **39**, 40, 42, **44**, 58, 80, 87

hagik-jin (Joseon 'crane's wing formation') 32, **51**, **52**, 55, **56**, 73, 80
Hansando Island **43**, **44**, 54, 56, 58, 84, 90, **92**
Hanyang 5, 7, 8–10, 12, 20, **39**, 43, 69, 82–83, 87
Happo **39**, 42
Hashiba Hidekatsu 22, 69
hwacha (Joseon wooden frame) **26**, **27**, 42
hyeopseon (Joseon small auxiliary boat) 32, 40–41, 59, 67, 85

Imjin War 4, 11–13, 16, **21**, 22, 24, **27**, **28**, 29, 35, 42, 51, **64**, 75, 83, 88–91
intelligence 6, 13, 24, 32, 40, 67
Ishida Mitsunari 21, 69
Iyo Province 22–23

janggunjeon (Joseon arrow missiles) 25, 60, 73, **81**
Janglimpo 67, **68**
Japan 4–6, 21–23, **34**, **35**, **36**, **59**, **60**, **67**, 84, 88
Japanese navy 5–6, 24, 32, **34**, 38, 40, 69, 75, 84, 87
Jeokjinpo **39**, 42–43
Jeoldosa (Joseon fleet commander/admiral) 11, 13, 16, 19, 24, **27**, 38
Jeolla Left Navy 11–13, 17–19, 24–25, **27**, 29, 38, **39**, 42, **44**, 53–54, 67, 73, 75, 80–81, **84**, 85, 87, 90
Jeolla Province 6, 7, 8, 11, 13, 20, 24, 37–38, 53, 65–66, 74, 82, 85, 87–88
Jeolla Right Navy 11–12, 16, 37, 43, 47, 54–55, 58, 67, 80–81, 85, 87
Jeong Bal 4, 5, 6
Jeong Un 17, **18**, 19, 38, 69, 73–74
Joseon 4–5, 6, 10–12, 14–15, 20–21, 24, **26**, **28**, 29–30, 36–38, **42**, 43, 45, 47, 50, 53, **54**, 55, 57, **61**, 66, 67, 73–74, **75**, 76, 77, 78, 80, **81**, 82, **86**, 87–88, 90–91
army 5, 7, 8, 20, 27, 33, 83, 87

arrows 58, 60, **80**
artillery **24**, 25, 59
court 24, 37, 53, 66, 74, 81–82, 84–87
fleet 5–6, 17, 19, 32, 42, 45, 54, 60, **61**, **64**, **68**, 69, **72**, 73, 76–77, 81–82, 85, 88
military 6, 10–11, 19, **28**, **31**, 75, 84, 86–89
navy 5–6, 10, 13, 15–16, 19, 24–26, **29**, **31**, 32, 34, 40, 42, 53, 55, 66, 68–69, **72**, 81, 86, 88
officers 10, **18**, 80, 84
ships 24, 29–30, 34, 45, 53–54, 57, 59–60, **64**, 73, 76, **79**, 80
troops 9, **18**, 27, **28**, **73**, 75, 77, 80
warships 25, 27, 69
Jurchens 11, 13, 16, 24, **27**

Kato Kiyomasa 7, 8, **21**
Kato Yoshiaki 21, **22**, 32, **64**, 69
Kim Deuk-gwang 17, 45, 75
Kim In-young 17, 40
Kim Song-il 5, 76–77
Kim Wan 17, 40
kobaya (Japanese small boats) 34, 51, **64**, **67**, 76
Kobayakawa Takakage 8, 66
Konishi Yukinaga 4, **6**, 7, 8, 9, 21, 74
  1st Division 4, 8
Korea 4–5, 14–15, 19–20, 23, 28, 32–34, **35**, **36**, 40, **41**, 42–43, 45, **46**, 50, 53, **59**, **64**, 66–67, **72**, 74–75, 77, 80–84, 87–88, 90
  Joseon Korea 15, 36, 38, 88
  Korean Peninsula 4–5, 83
  South 14, 15, 89, 91
Kuki Yoshitaka 21, 32, **35**, 53–54, **59**, **60**, **61**, **64**, **67**, 69, 75–76, **78**, 80
Kurushima Michifusa 32, 46
Kwak Jae-u 10, **76**, 77
Kwon Jun 17–18, 28, 45, 50, 57, 69, 73, 81, 87
Kwon Yul 9, 17, **66**, 82–83
Kyushu 32, 69
  campaign 19, 21–22

Lee Eon-ryang 17, 29, 69
Lee Gak 5, 6
Lee Gi-nam 29, 45, 51
Lee Mong-gu **78**, **79**, 80

Manho (Joseon port captain) 11–13, 17, 19
matchlock **27**, **36**
merchants 4, 35–36
Ming China 5, **21**, 36, 66
Mori Muriharu **51**, 52
munitions 25, 81, 83

Na Dae-yong 17, 19, 29–30, 33, 45
Nanjung Ilgi 14, **15**
naval bases 11, 25, 37–38
Nihon Maru 21, **34**, 35, 60–61, **64**, **65**, 67
Nokdo 11, 17, 19, 74
Nokdundo 12–13
Noryang 45, 54

O-atakebune (Japanese warship) **34**, **35**, 64
oars 28, 30, **31**, **41**, 50, 52
Oda Nobunaga 19, 21, 69
Okpo 11, **39**, 40, 90
Ozutsu teppo (Japanese arquebus) 35–36, **64**

panokseon (Joseon warship) 25, 28, **29**, 30, 40, **41**, 45–47, 50, **51**, 57–58, **59**, 60, **64**, 65, 67–69, **73**, 75–76, **77**, **79**, 80–81, **83**, 85
Park Hong 5–6, 37, 40
Pyongyang 7, 8–9, 74, 77, 82

reconnaissance 32, 34, 61
Righteous Army 27, 28, 66, 74, **76**, 77
  guerrillas 27, 66, 74, **76**
rivers 80, 87, **89**
  Gimhae 66, 85
  Imjin 7, 8, 74
  Nakdong 67, **68**
  Yangsan 66, 85
Ryu Seong-ryong 12–13, 82, 86

Sacheon 12, **44**, 45, 83
Sado 11, 17, 40
samurai 4, **20**, 22, 32, **33**, 52, 57, **64**, 76, 80, **89**
sekibune (Japanese warship) 34, 42, 46, 50, 51, 58, **64**, **67**, 76, 80
Seonjo, King 7, 16, 43, 74–75, 77, 86
Seungja chongtong (Joseon hand cannon) 27, **42**, 54

shields 34, **73**
  jangbangpae (Joseon, rectangular) **73**
  paengbae (Joseon, round) **73**
Shikoku 32–33, 69
shingijeon (Joseon rocket-propelled explosive arrows) **26**, 57
sieges:
  first siege of Jinju 9, 74, **76**
  second siege of Jinju 9, 89
Sin Rip 7, 8, **66**
Song Yo-chong 74, 86
submarines 16, 18–19
Suncheon 12, 16–17, **18**, **21**, 28–29, 38, 42, 45, 73, 85

tactics 5, 21, 24–25, 35–36, 88
Todo Takatora 21–22, **23**, 32, 40, 69
Tokugawa Ieyasu 21–23
Tokui Michiyugi 46–47, 50
Toyotomi (Hashiba) Hidekatsu 69, 74
Toyotomi Hidenaga 22–23
Toyotomi Hideyoshi 4, 19, 21–23, 74
Tsushima 5–6, 8, 75

Ukita Hideie 9, 53, 67
Ulsan 6, 12, 83
Ungcheon 12, 75, 77, 80–84, 91
Ungpo 74, 75–77, **79**, 80–85, 88

Wakizaka Yasuharu 8, 19, **20**, 21–23, 32, 53–55, **56**, 57, 58–59, 65–66, 69, 75–76, **78**, 80
Watanabe Shichiemon 20, 58
Won Gyun 5, 12, 14, 16–17, 19, 37–38, **39**, 40, 43, **44**, 45, 47, 53–55, **56**, 57–58, 65, 67, **68**, 73, 75, **78**, **79**, 80, 82, 84–86

Yangban (Joseon class) 10, 12
Yeonggwiseon 29, 45, 50, 51
Yi Eok-gi **16**, 38, 40, 43, **44**, 45, 47, **51**, 52, 54, **56**, 57–58, 67, **68**, 69, 73–75, 80, 85
Yi Il 13, 30, 37
Yi Sun-sin, Admiral 5–6, 8–9, 12, **13**, **14**, **15**, 16, **17**, **18**, 19–21, 24–25, **27**, 28–29, 30, 32–33, 36–37, **38**, **39**, 40–42, **43**, **44**, 45, **46**, 47, **50**, **51**, **52**, 53–54, 55, **56**, 57, 58, **59**, 60, **61**, **64**, 65–66, **67**, **68**, 69, **72**, 73–76, 77, 80–85, **86**, 87–90, **91**, **92**
Yulpo 11, **44**, 53